OUT

of the

BROOM
CLOSET

50 True Stories of Witches Who Found and Embraced the Craft

EDITED BY
ARIN MURPHY-HISCOCK

PROVENANCE
P R E S S

Adams Media
Avon, Massachusetts

DEDICATION

To all those who walk the path of alternative spirituality—publicly or privately.

Published by
Provenance Press®
an imprint of Adams Media, a division of F+W Media, Inc.
57 Littlefield Street, Avon, MA 02322. U.S.A.
www.adamsmedia.com
Provenance Press® is a registered trademark of F+W Media, Inc.

ISBN-10: 1-59869-891-5
ISBN-13: 978-1-59869-891-6

Printed in the United States of America.

J I H G F E D C B A

Library of Congress Cataloging-in-Publication Data
is available from the publisher.

This publication is designed to provide accurate and authoritative information
with regard to the subject matter covered. It is sold with the understanding that
the publisher is not engaged in rendering legal, accounting, or other professional
advice. If legal advice or other expert assistance is required, the services of a com-
petent professional person should be sought.
—From a *Declaration of Principles* jointly adopted by a Committee of the American
Bar Association and a Committee of Publishers and Associations

Many of the designations used by manufacturers and sellers to distinguish their
product are claimed as trademarks. Where those designations appear in this book
and Adams Media was aware of a trademark claim, the designations have been
printed with initial capital letters.

This book is available at quantity discounts for bulk purchases.
For information, please call 1-800-289-0963.

ACKNOWLEDGMENTS

My deepest gratitude goes out to all the contributors in this collection. Thank you for having the courage to talk about your pasts, your paths, and your thoughts on your experiences. Special mention goes to the ones who participated on a crazy deadline. You know who you are.

Andrea Norville hatched the idea; Kendra Vaughn-Hovey did some of the groundwork and handled the initial stage of the project; the anonymous copyeditors and proofreaders of Adams Media improved the product and made us all look fabulous.

TABLE OF CONTENTS

INTRODUCTION

Some of us call ourselves witches or Witches. Some of us call our selves Pagans, philosophers, humanists, or simply spiritual people. Others identify as Goddess-worshippers or Nature-honorers. Do the labels matter?

Sometimes they do. Sometimes we need a label to finally make sense of what we believe.

This anthology collects the first-hand experiences of real people as they discover, explore, and walk their Pagan paths. Whatever the word they have chosen to use to identify their spiritual choices, every single one of them is a regular, everyday person who has dealt with the pressure of self-identification, then identification within a larger com- munity—be it family, the workplace, or the public in general.

For most, the very first step of admitting to themselves they are Pagans is the hardest. In other words, candidly defining what they felt, dedicating themselves, or acknowledging in some way that this path, this faith, this spiritual way was their own, was the most difficult part. In effect, they came out of the broom closet to themselves. For some, once that first unveiling was complete, there was joy. For others, there was then a different kind of coming out required—to those around them.

Not everyone in this anthology has chosen to publicly identify him or herself as a follower of an alternate spiritual path. For some it isn't important—they consider spirituality a private and personal thing. Others identify themselves as Pagan only to other Pagans. Still others openly wear their religious symbols and demand time off for their holidays and festivals. Everyone's choice is different, as it should be. There are people whose stories talk about how they are comfortable with operating within two religions at once—one in their hearts, and the other socially. As Oisce puts it, "I believe that all gods are one god. I do not lie when I pray in the words of another religion because I believe." It is imperative to understand that every single contributor here, and every single reader, defines and deals with their spirituality in their own way. Taras Stasiuk clearly outlines that your questions and your answers are what count, not accommodating someone else's definitions and standards. For some, outlining the differences is what defines their path; for others, it is connecting the similarities.

There is a very wide range of paths and experiences illustrated in this book. Some of the names you might recognize; many you will not. Some people practice a very defined path; others are more free form. Different paths complement different lives; different avenues and practices provide the spiritual nourishment each of us seeks.

Despite the differences in paths and experiences, there are several common themes that surface again and again throughout these stories. One is the use of books to access or further knowledge. People read books and discover the existence of modern Paganism, or read in order to research this new spirituality to which they've been introduced in some way. These books aren't necessarily classifiable as New Age, either. Some read fiction, or mythology, or history texts and start to wonder if there's a modern analog.

Another common theme is the archetypal *coming home* sensation. After feeling out of synch, the practitioner discovers Paganism and feels as if it is what he or she has been looking for, or experiences a sense of comfort and belonging. Some people, such as Brenda Gibson, experience something moving and only later identify what the experience was. Ceri Young explains this feeling of coming home as being the relief of finally putting a name to all the different pieces of the puzzle that slowly collect throughout your life.

There are some unhappy commonalities as well. Some of the people in this anthology experienced brutal discrimination for their differences—sometimes physical violence, sometimes social discrimination. Some people have been disowned by their families due to their choices or actions deriving from those choices. They remain true to their personal choices while mourning their losses.

Sometimes the resistance or discrimination isn't from the non-Pagan community, but from within the Pagan community itself. Cerridwen Johnson writes about the prejudice she encounters from other Wiccans and Pagans when she reveals that she's Gardnerian. Blade writes about technopaganism, his preferred spiritual focus, and the resistance to the concept he has encountered within the Pagan community.

Some of the contributors found their spirituality expressed in unexpected parallel paths, such as science and philosophy. Sometimes the challenges aren't in the form of social or familial resistance, but in the form of how you define spiritual practice, and how you reconcile it to your expectation of what constitutes a spiritual life. People like Brendan Myers and Taras Stasiuk think and reason about aspects of their paths, concluding that the path they're each on is the answer for them as unique individuals.

Several community leaders share their experiences here. Gina Ellis weaves her observations of the evolution of public perception of and response to Wicca in Canada into a personal account of her journey along her Pagan path. Amanda Hyde talks about how her community organization skills led her to make contacts and act as a representative of the Pagan community in several different locations. It's a treat to see how these leaders present themselves, for it's thanks to people like them that alternate spirituality has become as widely accepted as it has today. Without them, this anthology wouldn't exist. We are deeply in debt to the groundbreakers and the ambassadors of our community, those who have gone before and those who still work to educate.

Many underline the fact that their faith is their own personal business. There's no need for them to point out what they are to everyone they meet. Others live lives that require them to wear their spirituality on their sleeves: shop owners, authors, celebrants, clergy, or teachers. There is no right or wrong way to live. Being out of the closet doesn't mean yelling about what you are from the rooftops; it means not actively hiding what it is you believe. How far each of us is comfortable with sharing that information depends on our lifestyles, our personalities, and our social environments. For example, Oisce is a Pagan author who publishes under her own name, but who is still relatively unknown in her home community. She is technically out of the closet, but hasn't made a point of bringing it to the attention of those around her because she respects them as well as her own beliefs. "It's not just about me," she writes, and she's right. A decision to come out of the broom closet, either selectively or fully, affects not only the individual who walks a Pagan path but those around him or her as well. Choosing who to reveal your beliefs and your spirituality to can be soul challenging. And again, there are no right answers; each of us must weigh the consequences and choose accordingly.

Many of the contributors I spoke to commented on how deeply revealing working on these stories was for them. It forced them to examine the origins of their faith, to evaluate how they have changed, and to put into words nebulous concepts and feelings. It's been a life-changing experience for me as well, as I've read through these stories of deep emotional impact, and seen what people have lived through and what they're still living through: the challenges, the transitions, the pride with which they move past obstacles, the pain with which they move through their lives forever altered by prejudice or rejection. The strength contained within these stories touches me deeply, and I know it will move you as you read them, too.

We can all hope for a day when spirituality isn't a divisive thing, when our actions and the way we live our lives say more about us than the word that tags our faith. Fortunately, many people in this collection point out that their journeys are still ongoing, that they encounter fresh challenges and new things to learn every day. Coming out—whether to oneself or to one's family or friends—is only the beginning. With every experience we must re-evaluate, integrate, and start anew. It's one of the blessings of our chosen spiritual path, and part of our ongoing relationship with the Divine.

Arin Murphy-Hiscock
Vernal Equinox, 2009

YES, WE ARE WORKING PROFESSIONALS

by Deb Goeschel

I hang sprigs of holly around my cubicle at Yule, and display a lava lamp at Midsummer. A small container of sea salt sits readily at hand for when the stress of deadlines leaks from my coworkers into my space. A ceramic fairy dressed in yellow perches on a bookshelf. A Goddess calendar hangs on one of the cubicle walls. A mini Goddess aromatherapy statue dispenser sits in front of my new flat-screen computer monitor right next to the rubber-ducky Witch. Being Wiccan at work hasn't been nearly as dramatic, or traumatic, as I thought it would be. It hasn't been painful, awkward, or tense. It's been ridiculously drama free . . . and I know how lucky I am.

When I started my current job, at a relatively small company, in a relatively small New England town south of Boston, I was out of the broom closet to my family and friends—had been for years. But I was still keeping my professional life and my personal/spiritual life quite separate. I couldn't comprehend how a marketing and communications professional could be received, accepted, and taken seriously if she was also openly Wiccan. This belief was initially upheld by an encounter with one of my coworkers shortly after I started my job.

I was in the women's bathroom washing my hands and I could see in the mirror my coworker repeatedly glancing down at the pentacle ring I'd worn for years. It's not large. It's not ostentatious, but it can't be mistaken for anything but what it is—a Pagan ring. It was, and is, the only Pagan/Wiccan jewelry I wear all the time. And I was having my first experience of someone actually noticing.

Looking and sounding extremely nervous and trepidatious, she said, "That's an interesting ring . . . what is it? A Star of David?"

I thought, "Oh my, here we go," and reached for the simplest answer, one which wouldn't put either of us in a combatant or defensive position.

"It's an ancient symbol of protection," I replied.

"Oh," she said with clear relief in her voice. "I thought it was . . . could be . . ." She gave a nervous laugh. ". . . the sign of the Devil or something."

I simply chuckled and told her it couldn't be because I didn't believe in the Devil, and the subject was dropped. And I kept very quiet about being Wiccan for several years. I didn't lie about it, but I didn't mention it. I remember when discussions around holiday plans and/or traditions would come up, there were a couple of times where my reply had to be, "I don't know. I don't remember, I'm no longer Christian," and the conversation would turn. This was fine for a time, but once I left my solitary path, dedicated myself, and went through formal first-degree training, I found I no longer wanted to live two lives. I wanted to be openly Wiccan at work . . . just like I was openly Wiccan with my family and friends.

An unfolding evolution best describes how I came to live openly as a Wiccan within my family and close circle of friends. There was very little outward drama. Of course, anyone who's been through a spiritual process understands how much inner drama occurs—peeling back the layers of consciousness, eliminating outdated belief systems, dismantling old and harmful patterns, and (re)discovering one's personal power and Divine connections rarely happens without a little internal drama, and frequently happens with lots of internal drama. I was no exception.

Although raised in the Roman Catholic tradition, my mother's example was not one of strict Church law. My Irish Catholic mother's first rebellion happened early—she married a Lutheran. And as I hit adolescence, she'd occasionally visit a medium. And I realized she didn't go to confession each and every week. Nor did she think psychics and Tarot readers were evil. She didn't condemn other religions. She thought sex was healthy—and fun. And she never believed she'd go to hell for any of these contrary beliefs and actions. Without meaning to, my mother provided me space to question the Church, setting the stage for me to begin looking outside of what I knew to find answers to questions I wasn't quite sure how to ask.

However, it wasn't until after a lot of upheaval in my mid-twenties, including a painful divorce (and subsequently moving back home with my parents) that I started my quest in earnest to find a spiritual home. I spent over a year church hopping, trying out different variations of Christianity until landing, with moderate satisfaction, in a Unitarian church. During this same time period, I'd also discovered a New Age/Wiccan supply shop and found myself wandering in more often than not. The inventory, the great smell of incense, and friendliness of the owner and staff all combined to make the store one of my favorite places . . . and they offered introductory classes in Wicca, which intrigued me. So, while I was learning through the Unitarian services that I actually missed the ritual of the Catholic mass, in these intro Wiccan classes I began to hear language that sounded familiar. I honestly can't remember how long this process of initial discovery was—one year? Two? But I do remember the day I realized that I'd unconsciously created an altar in my bedroom. This was the moment when I actively began to redefine who I was with regards to spiritual titles.

What followed were years as a solitary Wiccan, studying and learning about Wicca in general in whatever books my library and local bookstore carried, and about Wicca specifically as it related to me. Learning that I could create my own rituals to worship was an eye- and heart-opening experience. And most importantly, I found myself instinctively celebrating, meditating, communing, and connecting whenever I found myself in Nature. In a quandary over a decision? I'd go outside and meditate until the answer was clear. Want that new job? I'd go outside on the full moon and chant my wishes to Her . . . and I'd get the job. Want to say "thanks" for blessings and help? I'd go outside and whisper my thank yous to the wind. It was always outside where I found succor for my soul and prayers for and from my heart.

Throughout those initial years, I moved within my family dynamic as though Wicca was nothing more unusual than choosing to wear green on St Patrick's Day. My family accepted my "I'm going to a Wiccan class tonight" statements with the same indulgent tolerance they applied to any of my activities (theater, voice lessons, kayaking lessons, photography, rugby club, cake decorating, dating—the list goes on!), although I'm sure there was little-to-no understanding about how seriously I approached this particular subject. But as time went on, eventually Mom's Sunday morning question of "Are you going to church?" (which had been asked every Sunday since I moved home after my divorce) changed to only asking on major Christian holidays and, eventually, after many earnest conversations on my part, stopped with no real fanfare whatsoever. Mom was experiencing her own spiritual questioning and apparently figured she could no longer worry about mine.

My leap from openly Wiccan within my family to openly Wiccan with my friends came after I moved to Boston to get my master's in journalism. For the first time, I found myself wanting and needing more than what my solitary practice was offering—I wanted spiritual community. I found myself curious about group ritual—something I'd never experienced. Arsenic & Old Lace (now an online venue) was a Wiccan supply shop in Brighton that also housed the Pagan Community Center and often hosted open Sabbat rituals. Through these open rituals, I found myself growing more open about what I did to worship. I didn't take to proselytizing on street corners, or wearing Laurie Cabot-like robes in public, but I did wear my pentacle ring every day and I stopped thinking of my spiritual path as something alternative. So much so, that I inadvertently outed myself while working on a magazine article for which I was interviewing a Wiccan High Priestess. I simply thought it'd be an interesting feature article about someone and a topic that very few people know anything about. I wrote the article in first person, and it never occurred to me that by doing so, I was declaring to everyone who read the article that I was a regular participant in Wiccan ritual.

Through the years, I've always encouraged family and friends to ask questions. I told them as long as they asked with honest curiosity rather than prurient condescension, I'd answer whatever questions they wanted to ask. I partly believe that because I simply and very un-dramatically declared Wicca as my path, and never asked anyone, "What do you think of this?" or in any way implied I needed permission or—and perhaps most importantly—tried to convince everyone else Wicca was *the* spiritual answer—I created space in which my circle of friends and family could slowly get used to my choice and ultimately accept it. And I knew my family had finally, and truly, accepted my path—even if they did not fully understand it—when they were upset I didn't invite them to my first degree initiation! They were only slightly mollified when I explained a little bit about how small and personal that ritual was—not to mention it was held pre-dawn in the woods after a full night of rain—it wasn't like a public Catholic confirmation at all. Their reaction to this event told me everything I could ever hope for when it comes to family support. Realizing that my family understands how much I live my spirituality on a daily basis is a precious gift, which I do not take for granted. I'm blessed with their understanding, acceptance, and love. And these are the things that allow me to go to work and be openly Wiccan.

I still don't proselytize on the street or around the water cooler. I don't think religion is an appropriate conversation for the office. However, I do think it very important to be who I am in totality—a college-educated, mainstream professional woman, who never went through a rebellious teen period defined by Goth culture, who happens to practice Wicca. I'm as normal as anyone else. The only position I have with regard to Wicca is helping debunk the myth—when it comes up—that Wicca is a fringe religion. I want people to understand that Wiccans can be found amongst our doctors, lawyers, construction workers, waiters, social workers, police force, marketing and communication professionals, in fact, in any profession—it is not just a religion for the rebellious. Wicca offers me beauty, passion, courage, will, responsibility, community, tolerance, acceptance, surrender, and joy, all the things we all seek on our spiritual paths. So, when someone asks me something specific, such as, "What's the holly for?" I'll answer honestly and simply. And when a particularly inquisitive new coworker insisted (during a project meeting I was running last year) on knowing where I was spending my vacation, I told her, and everyone else who was listening, "I'm attending a large Pagan festival." And when her response was "That's so cool," followed by the outright question, "Are you Wiccan?" I answered the only way I knew how. I smiled and said "Yes," and then called our meeting to order.

EMPOWERED BY MY FAITH

by Debra Siegrist

As a solitary witch, I have turned to my faith for strength and have repeatedly been blessed with spiritual understanding and awakening. Whenever I experience low points in my life, my spiritual beliefs have always guided me through the rough spots, but never so much as when I almost lost my son.

I was sound asleep and suddenly awakened by the phone at 2:30 A.M. It was snowing pretty hard outside and I remember the trauma room nurse telling me to be very careful on the ride up to the hospital. I could hear and sense the urgency in his voice, but I still asked if it would be okay to wait until morning when the storm let up. He said, "I would really try to make it up here. It is touch and go." I felt my heart sink instantaneously and I was hoping, praying, that my son would please hold on until I got there to hold him. Steven and his twin brother were born in December of 1969. They were two months premature and weighed only 3 lbs. 2 oz. each. The doctor said it was highly unlikely that they would survive. After spending two months in the hospital with round-the-clock care, they finally came home. On my way to the hospital that dreadful stormy night, I couldn't help but think that he beat the odds when he was born, so maybe just maybe, he could beat them again thirty years later.

When I finally arrived at the emergency room, the trauma nurse explained that a bullet from a .357 magnum had ripped through his abdomen and severed his femoral artery and also did some damage to his intestines and other organs. I was told that he was lucky to have had five specialists working on him during his emergency surgery. I sat by his bedside listening to the sounds of machines beeping as they tried desperately to keep him alive. I bent over and whispered in his ear, "Mom is here, please come back to me, I love you." He squeezed my hand, but couldn't speak while hooked up to the respirator. I heard a still small voice inside of me say, "Lay your hands on him and I will work through you." I knew it was the Goddess speaking to me and I knew listening to Her was the only chance I had of healing my son. I trusted Her and began laying my hands on his body and praying to the powers of the Universe—the God and Goddess—to help me heal my son. I knew that they were listening and I knew that I was doing exactly what They wanted me to do. He had tubes coming out of everywhere and I could feel my heart beating wildly in my throat. I never felt so helpless, but I began whispering my healing prayers anyway. The nurse was concerned that his internal bleeding wasn't going to stop, but as I continued to pray I suddenly felt a strange sensation: A feeling as if there was an electrical current running though my entire body and then from my hands into his body. I could see the brown murky color of his dismal aura but refused to give up. In a short period of time, his vital signs started to improve and I collapsed into a chair in the corner of the room, completely drained of energy. I watched his aura change from brown to white, the color of God and Goddess energy. In that moment I just knew that he would recover.

No one in the hospital ever asked us what our faith was during his two week stay, but it didn't matter because my Wiccan faith is strong and I believed that it would carry me through this ordeal. Steven was released on Christmas Eve, just in time to celebrate the holidays, and the doctors were amazed at his recovery.

I have always felt empowered by my faith and it has brought me the strength and courage to survive life's darkest moments. Sometimes we forget to, or feel guilty when, we take time to nourish our own souls. It is not selfish to spiritually fill ourselves because we need that time to find the delicate balance in our lives. Only then can we truly be of service to others. I am so incredibly thankful that I had that knowledge and understanding before my son was shot.

An Exercise in Tolerance

by Joshua M. Thomas

"You're a what?" She began to cry over the phone.

"It's nothing like you see in movies or anything," I pleaded. "It's nothing bad or Satanic."

My words didn't seem to make her feel any better. I felt terrible and confused. I mean, I knew from past experiences that I would most likely have to give some explanations and reassurances when I opened up to my high school girlfriend of six months, but tears? That was unexpected. Until then, I had only told Amanda and her parents that my mother was Catholic and my father was Jewish. I just avoided discussions on religion. "I'm going to have to tell my mom," she said in between sobs.

Well, I guess I expected that much. "Okay, if you want," I replied.

Who was I to say no? I felt ready to answer any questions and criticisms her parents would throw at me. Besides, I had been getting along with Amanda's mother well. I participated in church events and sat in on youth group meetings. Her mother had already told me how highly she thought of me. I even went on an overnight trip with

Amanda and her family to an annual Lutheran youth-group convention a couple of months prior. I was confident that we would be able to work things out.

I was very content with my spirituality. I had first discovered Wicca while in middle school and identified with it not only spiritually, but morally. I decided to declare it as my faith only after several years of research had proved to me, without a doubt, that it was right for me.

The conversation with her mother the next day was a two-hour boxing match. She threw sharp accusations at me while I tried to defend myself, reasoning against her tirade of blows. She yelled at me about how I had lied to both her and Amanda by keeping my faith a secret from them. I explained to her that I merely wanted to avoid any prejudice from them. I did not want to reveal my religious choice until I felt comfortable that they knew me well enough that they would not jump to any hasty conclusions. She was not sympathetic to my reasons. She came up with brilliant excuses for dismissing everything I had to say in defense of myself and my religious choice. By the end of it, I was exhausted and emotionally drained. Her words had cut deeply.

Over the next few months, Amanda was still uncomfortable with Wicca, but looked past it while we were together; her mother didn't shift her stance on the issue. Even so, she decided she would not restrict her daughter from seeing me. I attended Amanda's softball games, and was invited into their home. Her mother also decided to take those opportunities to relentlessly remind me of how I was influenced by the Devil. She often remarked, "You're bringing Satan into our lives."

I kept in mind part of the Wiccan Rede that states, "speak ye little, listen much," as I listened patiently to her concerns and harsh accusations of Wicca, while I was at their house for dinner or was accompanying them to an event. I knew I had to stay strong and not lower myself to anger and malice. I reminded myself of the threefold law and how the energy you put out comes back three times greater. That, and the Wiccan Rede, discouraged me from speaking back in anger and comforted me knowing that her negativity would come back in my favor. So, I kept my head up and stayed positive. I tried offering some explanations on Wicca, things I had learned over my years of study and I suggested books for her to research. She would dismiss these as a ploy of Satan's to deceive her while expressing pity that I was probably unaware of it.

"I have to let God guide my decision," she would say.

I couldn't help but be amused when a few weeks later she showed me a book that she had recently bought about Witchcraft. It turned out to be one I had already read several years earlier and was among one of my favorites. She certainly was not amused when I pointed this out to her.

She also set certain rules that she asked me to follow. When I was at their home or in her car, I could not wear my pentagram necklace, a small and discreet pendant that I wore almost daily to school. I agreed to this without any complaint, after all I was a guest at her home and in her car, so, if that was what she wished, I would oblige. She also insisted that I attend church with them on Sundays. I understood that relationships require compromise, but I refused to attend every Sunday. Instead I agreed to go every other week. I didn't feel it was right for her to try to make me go to church with them, and I certainly didn't enjoy waking up early on Sundays to sit for an hour bored out of my mind. However, I looked on the bright side and went anyway to prove to them that I took Wicca seriously and could not be chased away from Amanda or my religion. Besides, I got to spend some extra time with her family and I knew it would help to ease any concerns.

I saw the ongoing conflict with Amanda's mother as perhaps my greatest mental, spiritual, and moral test as a teenager. I was not going to leave the girl I cared for simply because of her mother's convictions, nor would I let her turn me away from my faith. I was not going to let her negativity make me less friendly, or let her ignorance make me afraid to learn and experience. I was going to stand strong and prove to myself, Amanda, and her mother, that negativity was not going to stop me from being happy, or from being who I wanted to be, or from being with whom I wanted to be with. It was not going to stop me from believing what I believed in.

Amanda and I stayed in a relationship for another five months after I revealed I was Wiccan. I became a senior in high school and eventually Amanda and I broke up. When I graduated from high school we grew further apart. I'm proud to say that the conflict over my religion was not a reason why we ended our relationship. Religion should never cause conflict in peoples' lives, and I had worked hard to make sure it didn't get between us. I don't regret staying with Amanda while her mother berated me about my religion. In fact, I am glad for it. I'm sure that my actions gave Amanda and her family some more understanding and respect for Wicca. Those eleven months were filled with tears, fun times, conflict, love, and new experiences. It made me a stronger individual and taught me important things about myself and how to handle my religious choice in social situations. It strengthened my bond with Wicca and my spirituality, because I proved to myself that I could not be swayed from the path that I knew was right for me. For those reasons, I thank Amanda for sticking by me, and I thank her mother for what I learned and also for the kindness and generosity she showed me amidst her often demeaning and unfair remarks toward me. I know it was not easy for Amanda, or easy for her mother to let her only daughter date someone Wiccan, but she stuck by what she thought was right, and so did I.

Not on the Syllabus

by Ashleen O'Gaea

When I met him for the first time, the God was dancing like Tom Bombadil.

That's how I recall it, anyway; it might have been just his corduroy jacket open and flapping in the breeze. I was standing on a college campus lawn in a freshman registration line. He was an associate professor, and when he stopped to chat with me and a new-met friend, he called himself "a moral anarchist." Yikes! I'd been raised by emotionally conservative parents who were afraid of a smile's shadow, so he terrified me.

But I had to take humanities class from him, and during the part of the course that covered Anglo-Saxon times and culture, I had a very unusual experience. As the professor read to us in Old English, I suddenly understood every word, and when he finished and resumed speaking in modern English, I heard it as gibberish! It took me several minutes to come back again.

When I read his obituary in the alumni magazine just a few years ago, it hit me: the late Prof. Webb—Webb of Wyrd?—had been an avatar of the God! I hadn't been prepared to meet him then, but memory held the introduction in trust until I was ready.

The Goddess first got my attention as I was writing my junior qualifying exams. We had several hours to complete them, and though I was a townie and could've gone home to compose my essay answers, I chose to ensconce myself at a booth in the campus coffee shop. I opened my exam book, smoothed the first page—and was overwhelmed by an anxiety attack. One segment demanded an identification and discussion of a line from Shakespeare, and I hadn't any idea which play, much less which act and scene. Another challenged me to analyze a poem that made no sense to me. My mind was blank, and I felt numb all over. I resigned myself to doom.

As I stared at my empty pages, barely feeling the pen in my hand, I became aware of a golden light, and of music. I looked around, but no one else seemed to be aware of the hazy glow or the harp-like music. Before I could wonder what it meant, answers to the exam questions came to me, clearly and concisely, and stayed with me long enough for me to write them down! I passed the exam, and all I could call it then was a miracle. Now I call it an encounter with the Goddess, a blessing, a sign, one of the first notes of my call to Priestess-hood.

A wave of fairly flippant occultism was sweeping the country then, and like many others, my campus found it amusing. At our Renaissance Faires there were booths where you could sell your soul to the Devil for a dollar (and get it back again by doing some volunteer work). I avoided those, but I read Tarot, and played Ouija, and found myself involved with a group of friends that included a self-styled *bad witch*.

My semester-long witch war with her, its details long forgotten, gave me my first confidence in the psychic powers I'd both taken for granted and worried about. A few other incidents seemed significant, too, but when I left school to get married, all that faded.

My husband, Canyondancer, and I were married in my Unitarian Universalist church, where I'd learned a lot that's still useful about mainstream and obscure religions during my Sunday school years. As we rehearsed the wedding ceremony, the organist disapproved of our choice of music (the "Bridal Chorus" from Wagner's *Lohengrin*, and Mendelssohn's "Wedding March") as too Pagan; he played it beautifully anyway.

We were Unitarians a little longer; we attended the Unitarian church in Tucson until its governing board's decisions became intolerable to a fair number of the congregants. Then, with some of the others, we formed a fellowship that focused on celebrating the Solstices and Equinoxes, the beauty and power of the seasons, and the holiness of the natural world. When the fellowship dissolved as its members moved on, my husband and I continued to mark the Solstices and Equinoxes, knowing that they (along with Halloween and May Day) were the Pagan foundations of modern Christian holidays.

But not until I read Starhawk's *The Spiral Dance* and Margot Adler's *Drawing Down the Moon* was I aware of a context in which both our reverence for Nature as the source of sacredness and the occult episodes of my high school and college years could make sense. Understanding that the sensational bits weren't the whole or even the main content of the religion that accepted them was a relief, satisfying and empowering. So was the realization that our spiritual orientation was shared by tens of thousands of others, and that it had a name: Wicca.

The first time I was interviewed about Wicca was on the radio, and you could hear the pages of prepared remarks rustling in my trembling hands the whole time. I can't say that I began by embracing my fears, but I did at least shake hands with them. And because I wasn't going to get fired or evicted, be harassed by the neighbors or see our son removed from our home for being out of the broom closet, I closed its door behind me and threw away the key.

Religion didn't come up much in our long-distance conversations with our relatives, most of whom lived about 1,500 miles away. I don't think Canyondancer's mother ever knew, although given that she was a participant in some of my occult experiences, I can't think she'd have minded. Once we assured his father and stepmother that they could still send us Christmas cards, they had no further questions; one of 'dancer's brothers was a member of our first coven. My parents accepted our Paganism for the shock value it had among their friends! (I do remember getting a phone call, though, after Mom saw a *Tonight Show* episode on which a guest had mentioned something about celebrating the Summer Solstice by running around naked, burning money. I told her I wished we had money to burn, and we both laughed.)

The cliché is that after that, we never looked back. And we didn't, in the sense that we no longer felt like trailblazers, because we saw then that the trail had been marked and was blazing before us, and that we had many companions on our path. We have never since doubted our religious commitment or had a crisis of faith. We have grown in Wicca and are now full-fledged liturgical and pastoral clergy, still called and challenged to grow, personally and professionally.

But in another way, I often look back, and find doing so both agreeable and important. For the last thirty years and more we've been blessed and darned lucky—is there a difference there?—to live in Tucson, where it's pretty safe to be Pagan. I worked for almost twenty years for an attorney who was not only tolerant, but proud of my "Witchism," as she called it. I felt beholden then, and am still inclined now, to dedicate my freedom of religion to those who, hobbled by other people's ignorance or their own fear, haven't attained it yet.

This sense of duty, if you will—duty I swore to the God/dess in the first Wiccan oath I took—has led me to volunteer, since the summer of 2000, for Mother Earth Ministries-ATC, a Neo-Pagan prison ministry (as a priestess and mentor, I answer over fifty letters a month from inmates all over the country), and led me to overcome a natural and parentally nurtured shyness and clumsiness, a fear that I'll sing off-key (which I still occasionally do, but I don't think twice about taking the risk now), and an ineptitude for extemporizing that I'm still working on. Looking back, and beholding that the Goddess has indeed been with me from the beginning, is one of the ways I keep the Charge real for myself, and myself real for the gods.

For years now, my comfort in Wicca has been so great that there isn't a broom closet big enough to hold it. But this is only true because the Goddess and God recognized my true will before I did, and took me into their hearts before I was plucky enough to reach out to them. Now, I do my best to share their embrace with the world.

THE CELEBRATION OF LIFE AND REBIRTH

by Lynette C. Mansani

I have always longed for something different, something more in my life, something that could fill me at the very core of my being. I longed for a relationship with God but was unable to find it in the Catholic Church, which I was raised in. My mother once told me that everyone needs to believe in something, because without faith, the world would be in chaos. I have always remembered those words and hoped that she would understand when I found a faith that was right for me and wasn't Catholicism.

I wanted happiness my whole life, but I just kept looking for it in all the wrong places. I thought people could fill my void until I met the Goddess. The day I met her was the day I took a mythology class in high school. When I learned about her, everything came together for me and it was a huge *ah-ha* moment in my life. Battling depression and anxiety has always been a challenge for me, but I am in such a better place than I was back then and I owe it all to the Goddess.

As I searched for what I would major in at college, the strangest thing happened. I started to understand the connection to the God and Goddess. I found information about Faerie Wicca online, and once again, I experienced such an incredible *ah-ha* moment. I grew up loving dragons and faeries! In searching for the fey in books and on the Internet, I found the true meaning of Wicca. It wasn't evil and there was no such thing as the Devil or Hell! After having all of these experiences, one on top of the other, I knew Wicca was what I had always been looking for.

It all came together for me in the summer of 2006. The birth of my son, Aidan, in June, finding a sympathetic Wiccan congregation in July, and landing a better job in August made my summer nothing less than spectacular. All of these experiences, but especially the birth of my son, became an affirmation of the religious beliefs that I hold so close to my heart today. Giving birth was an experience that helped me fully grasp the level of importance the God and Goddess have in my life. Having Aidan was nothing less than a deeply spiritual and fully magical experience. It brought me so much closer to the Mother Goddess! During childbirth, I felt her love flowing through me and I knew that with the pain of every contraction she was with me. Everything was going to be okay. In that most incredible day of my life She gave me the responsibility of caring for her creation, which brought meaning to my life. The connection I immediately felt to my new baby boy was like nothing I had ever experienced in my life. Every time I looked at my precious infant's face, or looked into his eyes, or counted his fingers and toes, I saw the God and Goddess. I was so incredibly joyful and thankful for the gift they had given me.

The day we brought Aidan home from the hospital, I noticed how crisp the summer air was. I knew I was glowing, and others made mention of how great I looked. The sky was bright blue with a few puffy white clouds. I thought I smelled flowers in the air, but didn't notice any around me. The trees rustled in the wind. I was overwhelmed with thanks and had no idea how to express it. Aidan was very healthy, and even though I was tired, I viewed life differently and found myself thinking so positively. The Goddess heard my gratitude and sent me a warm breeze to tell me that I could always trust her. I know now that day had a huge personal and spiritual impact on my life. There was no denying that I had deepened my connection with the Goddess for the rest of my life.

A few weeks later, I saw statue of Isis nursing her son, and I found myself identifying with that statue as a new mother who was also nursing my son. It symbolized a spiritual awakening, and a rebirth of my own.

A BATTLE WORTH FIGHTING

by Anda Powers

It was the most frightened I'd ever been in my life, lying on the pavement and looking up into the faces of three older boys. I knew that I had made a big mistake sharing my faith with my boyfriend (now ex-boyfriend). His cousins and friends were laying down their sadistic cards, while they threatened to beat and rape me. "You're a Witch," one of them spat. "You deserve it."

I had found Wicca many years before, after walking Christian and Native American paths. For as long as I could remember, I felt spiritually excluded, confused and dissatisfied. My constant questions were more than an annoyance to my Sunday school teachers. They each became frustrated and quit their jobs. While I tried to live a devout Christian life, I was terrified of the vengeful God my pastor described. Each night, I prayed to keep my family safe, naming every terrible scenario I could think of while begging for mercy, until finally, exhausted, I fell asleep. I was still in grade school when my mother converted to Native American beliefs. I followed, finding a sense of comfort in a kind God and a fascination in animism and animal lore. I became more comfortable with death and no longer felt that crushing fear each night before bed. Still, my heart searched for something more.

I began to write poetry to express my yearning and steadily growing love of nature. Finally, I heard the voice of the Goddess. My older brother had bought a book about Wicca, but never read it. I whisked it away and read it voraciously. The Divine Feminine spoke to me. She told me that I wasn't alone, and that my feelings of discontent weren't evil or ungrateful. She gave me a gentle nudge toward the right path. I shared the book with my mother, who was very supportive. After reading it, she decided it was safe, and allowed me to explore the religion. I eventually dedicated myself to Wicca. My immediate family knew and although there was tension between my father and me, we grew into understanding one another. When I shared my beliefs with friends, more often than not, they quietly left me. One dragged me into a counselor's office, worried about my soul. Boyfriends decided I was crazy and teachers laughed at me. But as I got older, it became harder and harder to hide my views. Wicca had become a part of me and often came out subtlety in class discussions. I learned to deflect stares by admitting to being a hippie. Then a boyfriend relayed my faith to his closed-minded buddies and that's the day that I found myself in the parking lot of a local grocery store. As the fear overtook me and I was gasping for breath, the boys made their threats and then finally walked away, laughing. I consulted with a school counselor, who suggested that the incident didn't really happen. My feelings of helplessness and fear quickly converted into anger. Why can't I be a witch and be safe? In a moment of defiance, I pulled my small pentacle out of my t-shirt.

For the rest of my high school career, I endured death threats, mocking jokes, and the indifference of the administration. Kids didn't want to be my friend. Adults didn't trust me. But I felt that it was more important to be true to myself. I wanted to send a message that intimate interaction with the Goddess was more fulfilling to me than superficial interaction with people who couldn't accept me for who I am. Once again, I found solace in the pages of notebooks. I filled them with the glory of nature and attempted to align my hormonal, angst-filled, teenage life. I also found a few special people who looked past my differences and accepted me entirely. In a way, in coming out of the broom closet, I chose to endure those unique abuses and gained more solid friendships in return. I've never put my pentacle away and, in fact, received a larger pendant as a gift from my ever-supportive mother. I work a visible job where I'm often given tracts or lectures. Some people avoid me altogether or gossip about my "Devil star" with other employees. Customers have spat on me, prayed for me, and yelled at me, while coworkers have staged miniature interventions. I struggle to keep a calm tone and explain myself clearly. Sometimes it works, and sometimes it doesn't. When it doesn't, I am content to accept tracts and small Bibles, tossing them in the trash, or giving them to someone who can use them.

As for my notebooks, I still have many of them. Poetry is close to my heart. But I've also ventured into prose and am now a published Pagan author. What was once a way to deal with my world is now a way to share it with others. I began to wear my pentacle out of anger, but it has become a symbol of hope for me. I have a niece who is being raised in a Pagan-friendly household and there's always a possibility that the Goddess will speak to her as she grows. Every person I educate is one that will understand her better. Every battle I fight paves the way for her to be a Witch, and to be safe. In the end, that's what we all want. But in order for that to happen, some of us have to be public in an unsafe world. Some of us have to be willing to be uncomfortable, hurt or frightened. It is a holy sacrifice that becomes a part of us, like the Mother's touch in the rain.

How to Be a Pagan Author while Staying In the Broom Closet

Oisce

Closets are funny places. They can be places to hide, tucked in away with all the other bits and pieces that shouldn't be seen. They are safe places, secluded, dark like the womb, and quiet. They are places where you can listen to what's happening on the other side of the door without being exposed to it. They are places to escape what is happening on the other side. Memories are kept in closets, stored in boxes and draped over hangers, the things we want to hold onto but that have no current usefulness or are out-of-date; we might need them again one day so we store them away. In the closet, you can dream dreams, write poetry by torchlight, and sometimes, just sometimes, the closet is the entry to another world, a Narnia, a place of magical encounters and heroic adventures.

And the people who know us best, who know our secrets—those people know where to find us. Sometimes they might even join us in the dark while we whisper our secrets to each other, and share our arcane wisdom and create our own little world.

Is it any wonder I want to stay in the closet?

But all that thinking and dreaming and writing becomes something I want to bring out into the light. I have things to say and do that will make a difference to the world on the other side, and I love that world. Holy Mother Terra is my Narnia, my place of enchantment and wonder and heroic purpose. It is in this world that I find the dilemmas of good and evil, friends and foe, and everything on the edge of ultimate destruction or resurrection. So I want to step out of the closet and fly—but if the people of Terra see me flying about on my broom, they are likely to burn me and how can I speak then?

I live in a very small rural town with a couple of hundred people. The nearest urban center is half an hour's drive away, with a population of about 20,000. I have grown up in this area: we are third generation in the cemetery, and according to Australian folk tradition that makes us locals. I come from a big family who have been actively involved in nearly every type of social and work activity there can be had in such a place. We are well known. What I do, what any of us does, has repercussions not just for the individual but for the family and friends, and I've no wish to cause them hardship or grief unnecessarily.

I teach professional and creative writing (including subjects about mythology and symbolism) and my rule is that we talk about the writing, not about students' personal beliefs. We might discuss how mythology is shaped by and shapes the cultures, what it means for its adherents and storytellers, but not what we personally believe about any of it. We clarify definitions, and I will always make sure that the terms *Wiccan* and *Pagan* are explained if and when they arise, which is fairly often, but I don't come out.

The reason I give for this rule is that the classes are about stories and writing, not religious debate about who is right and wrong. If they want to hold those sorts of discussions, I encourage them to do it outside the classroom. By removing the contention in the classroom, there is a lot of learning about other religions and walks of life. The learning takes place by simply listening to the stories. But my students don't know they are being taught by a witch, and, if they did, some of the Christian students would be horrified. And they would discard all their learning as the Devil's soft deception.

I also work as a civil celebrant for weddings, naming ceremonies, and funerals. I provide individualized ceremonies that include whatever religious content the people want, making sure it is in accord with their beliefs, not mine. It is work that is very precious to me, especially the funerals, and work that I would not be able to do if I were labeled a Pagan (except for specifically Pagan ceremonies).

My partner's parents are devout Catholics and I've been to Mass with them and given readings and administered communion—a special role for which I have been anointed. Catholicism is a big part of my heritage, part of my personal history that I treasure very much, but they would feel deceived and betrayed if they saw me with my broom. I would be ostracised as well as excommunicated, and they would try to break up my relationship with their son. I asked my partner what he would say to them if they found out, and he said he would tell them

I was the same person they have known and liked all these years, no different. I love him for that.

The reason I asked him was because the second edition of my book, *Sunwyse: Celebrating the Sacred Wheel of the Year in Australia*, was coming out, but with a previously unused bio I'd provided to the publisher in another context included inside, a bio that identified the author as Pagan. It hadn't been in the revised proofs I'd corrected, and when I saw it I was horrified. I had carefully managed to keep this identity hidden for so long, even when the first edition came out, because the book includes aspects from a wide variety of religions and traditions rather than focusing on one and talks about relating these practices to natural cycles. People, including my partner's parents, knew that I was interested in other religions and that I did things differently, but not that I was a Pagan. My partner gave his parents a copy of the first edition the year that it came out, but I'm fairly certain that they flicked through it and never picked it up again. It's not their thing. They have come to Solstice celebrations at my place, where I get the children to run around with me and beat the boundaries, or where we bash a piñata-style scapegoat, or pick out blessing stones, or hang gifts for the faeries on the Faerie Tree—but they don't realise that's Pagan. They just think it's a seasonal party and I'm happy for it to be that way.

I was scheduled to have a public book launch for the new edition of *Sunwyse*. I feared that if the local paper read the revised bio and used it, I would be in real trouble. I was panicked, and my gut was churning; I ran through all the possible scenarios in my head. But nobody noticed it except for the ones who already knew.

It's a strange situation, that I can be a well-known Pagan author but still live in the closet within my home community. I was a regular contributor to *Witchcraft* magazine for years before it ceased operations, and it was a magazine readily available in general news agencies, but the only ones who bought it were those interested in witchcraft. I've written for the Faith column in a state-wide newspaper, but I write about the spirituality of nature and that's generally understood as something to which everybody can relate, not only Paganism.

Nobody notices the broom, unless they're other riders or it is pointed out to them. I have a blatant altar in the old fireplace of my kitchen, in full view of anyone who visited. But non-Pagans just did not notice it, even though it was covered with magic paraphernalia and images or statues of the Goddess in all her aspects, and some of the God. My father-in-law even looked at it one time and asked if I wanted him to unblock it so it could be used as a fireplace again. I said no, I liked storing things there! But others have recognized it straight away and we've nicked into the closet for a quick whispered conversation.

Coming out in any way other than I already have would be a huge statement and create extreme chaos. Some would never forgive me. If it was just for me, if I would lose my work, my reputation, my place in the community, and even face physical retribution because there would be a lot of anger. I could pay the cost if I felt that it would make a difference to the way that Paganism is viewed and understood. But it's not just about me. It's my family, my friends, and my partner who would also pay the price. And the people I have done funerals for, who would feel I had tainted something sacred. The Christian woman whose son (a good friend of mine) died recently, was grateful that even though it was not a church ceremony we could still include readings from their Bible. She would be devastated to be told I was a witch.

Do I deceive them by not being open about my true beliefs? No, but they would not always understand that. I believe in religion, I believe in religious expression, and I believe that all gods are one God. I do not lie when I pray in the words of another religion, because I believe. And, outside of the classroom, I do talk openly about what I believe: that all religions are a search for the truth, as well as a way of evading truths; and that while I value my Catholicism I am at odds with many of the Church's teachings. It is known that I read Tarot, practice meditation, and go to alternative festivals. I do not hide who I am, but I don't wear the labels of witch or Pagan unless I am with others who mean the same thing as I do when they use those terms.

I think I actually make more of a difference by being less confrontational and just presenting a different way of living. People know me by the way I live my life, not by the labels I wear, and that means we can hold all sorts of conversations and learn from each other in a way that would not happen if there were the walls of ignorant prejudice between us.

And for those who know the secrets of my closet, I bind them to keep those secrets. If I want someone to know my personal beliefs, then I will tell them myself. Some friends think this is too fear based and that I should be more open. I am afraid. I remember the Burning Times. I don't want to burn. I don't want my family to burn.

I tread carefully along my tightrope and make what difference I can, small inroads that erode people's prejudices and ignorance, or allow insight that challenges people to rethink their entrenched ideology. *Sunwyse* is written in such a way that it can be used by people of any spirituality or religion who are interested in a closer connection with Earth. And I celebrate the Sabbats with an eclectic mix of people, some of whom know only that they are celebrating the seasons. It's enough.

I would lose all of that freedom, and that ability to communicate these ideas to the broader community if I were labeled as a witch or Pagan. My closet would be broken down and used for firewood and it would be a lonely sky that I flew in if I were able to escape. I hope, I pray, that one day there will be the religious freedom to celebrate my religion more openly. But even then, I think I would still want to keep my closet, because it is a private place, a retreat, and I like the peace and quiet and wonder of the dark, hidden recesses that it offers me. I am now, and will remain, a closet dweller. Blessed be us all!

A MEANS TO PEACE

by Richard J. Goulart

Any journey begins by taking the first step, which is exactly how mine began. As a child, I felt drawn to something I would later in life know as metaphysics, without understanding what that really meant at the time. I used to spend hours visualizing, concentrating, and perhaps even meditating, without even realizing what I was doing. This had led me to my very first steps upon, or at least toward, my Wiccan path.

My personal journey into Wicca began in the early 1980s, when I found my way to a bookstore looking to start a serious spiritual journey. I remember how clearly I was drawn to *Buckland's Complete Book of Witchcraft*. I was a lost soul with a thirst for spirituality and only a few dollars in my pocket. It was one of the most exhilarating experiences I can remember as I felt a new door opening up for me. Although I knew of the occult and the esoteric nuances of Pagan practices, this book was my introduction to a "religious" side of Wicca, which later spawned my birth as a solitary practitioner.

I was intrigued by the magical aspect of this faith and the promise of some kind of personal control over my life and I immediately connected to the earth-based aspect of Wicca. It resonated deeply within me, especially since it was in harmony with my Native American heritage. In fact, the more I delved into the theology and teachings of Wicca, the more the two seemed to be forming a unified trail upon which I could travel to find my path to the Divine. This was, it seemed to me at the time, a perfect union, and one in which I was sure to find my spiritual self. It was a formula for enlightenment, peace, and love.

As time went on, however, I was having a harder time finding the spiritual side to my Wiccan practice. I felt alone and many of the books I read focused too much on the supernatural and the material, and not nearly enough on how to maintain a spiritual state of existence. For me, this was the most important side of any faith and the one that seemed most rooted in my Native American heritage. I was drifting further and further from the God and Goddess, and thus, away from my spiritual core.

A few tragedies occurred in my life as I became lost in my spiritual quest. The death of my mother and father, as well as a dear friend, left me numb and alone. I had become so mired in my grief that I was unaware and under-appreciative of all of the amazing gifts that the God and Goddess had bestowed upon me. I knew what I wanted—a strong and deep connection to the divine—but the day-to-day issues that seemed to be piling up were keeping me away from it.

Somehow, despite my lack of attention to them for so long, the God and Goddess called to me and gave me direction through the bleakest of times. My wife, discouraged by our surroundings and finally overwhelmed by the dark cloud that enveloped me, had left me for another man. Since she was the primary provider of the family, I was in a position where I felt that I had no real means of supporting myself and my two young sons. Yet somehow, at that moment, I knew, whether intuitively or through divine intervention (as if they are not one in the same), that I was not alone and, in fact, that I *was* in Their hands. An unusual sense of calm and peace had come over me, knowing that I could finally reconnect with my Pagan path. From that point on, a series of amazing events took place that could only be explained later as a testimony toward the existence of the God and Goddess. I began to see a pattern of occurrences spring from nowhere, and somehow, each and every one seemed to be crafted to help me on my journey.

First, my part-time job, which I had held for just over a month, seemed to be threatened by the added burden of having no one to take care of the children in the evening. This, the first of my concerns, was almost immediately put to rest by the response of my supervisor and his boss, both of whom assured me that whatever flexibility I needed they would provide. Then, within two months, they offered me a full-time position, and again assured me that they were aware and sympathetic to my situation.

Second, I found support from places I had no reason to expect it would come from, as my father-in-law and mother-in-law assured me that they were there if I needed them. My wife's sisters also helped ease the burden of both childcare and the lingering pain that the separation caused me.

Third, while the bond between my sons and I had always been strong, the ensuing months saw those relationships grow to nearly indefinable levels of love, compassion, and understanding. Because of the circumstances, we had grown to rely on one another and found, beyond a shadow of a doubt, how much we could count on each other.

Fourth, and finally, I had quiet time on those weekends when my children were staying with their mother. It was then that I listened. I listened to everything that helped me find the healing that protected me and allowed me to remain unscarred by the endless events that had hurt me so deeply. The God and Goddess watched over me in this time and called to me once again in my time of need.

My belief in the God and Goddess became overwhelmingly certain, however, thanks to one specific event. If I had any doubt up to that point, it was immediately gone after this experience.

I had been out to the store and was returning home on an early-March afternoon. The weather was cloudy, but not horribly cold or dreary. My mood was perhaps more so. I reached my door and began to unlock it. At that instant, Vega, the man my wife left me for, began yelling at me from about twenty feet or so away, and into the courtyard of the complex. As I walked over toward Vega, his glance darted in several directions behind me. I knew then what was happening. I sensed we were not alone and then saw a number of other men emerging from the shadows and beginning to creep closer toward me, encircling me. There was no mistaking their intent, as they were all his friends. I had met them once before briefly in the past. I readied and steeled myself for the confrontation, knowing that I had no opportunity for victory, when suddenly, the door to my apartment opened and my youngest son, Jason, came scampering out and ran to embrace me. I saw Vega motion to the mob, and they relaxed and stopped, not wanting to put my son in danger.

Two things showed me the protection I had been enveloped in by the God and Goddess. The first was the sudden and unexplained arrival of Jason, my son, who at four years old had still not mastered the unlocking and opening of the child-proofed door and knob. And second, and upon reflection now even more amazingly, was the sudden humanity and concern these men filled with evil intent had shown over the presence of a young child. Without Jason's arrival, I would have suffered at the very least a severe beating, and possibly much more. Jason and divine intervention prevented what was about to happen. The God and Goddess modified the circumstances and protected everyone involved. Now, that is a means to peace!

While this circumstance jumps out at me now, I can recall and relate countless other times when They were there. No bargaining, and certainly no devotion worthy of Their unrelenting and unwavering love has ever been expressed from me to warrant that devotion from Them. It simply *is* Their nature, Their essence, Their beauty, even for those of us who have spent their own time finding reasons to ignore Them, or at best, to give a degree of lip service to Them. The longer I live, the more I see Them in everything around me, above me, under me, and within me. That is the perfection of Them, for They are everything. And even when we fail to acknowledge Them, or love Them, They are always there, and always waiting to enfold us in the totality of Their love.

It's Just a Knowing

by Paul McVicker

I was raised in a small town in Northern Ireland and the church held a very big part in my family's life. I'm Irish and was christened a Catholic. As a young teen, I found myself afraid of God because of the teachings in the Bible. Each passing day grew more and more difficult for me, knowing that I was gay and the Bible taught that gay people had no place in our faith; that being gay was sinful. I couldn't understand why, if I was made in God's image, I was not accepted. It was so confusing. I know what they say, that at fourteen years old how could I know for sure? But I am an old soul and already knew so much about the world. I was sure that I was gay, but not so much that I was Catholic. During that time, I couldn't help but think that maybe I shouldn't have been born at all or that maybe there was something wrong with me.

Then one day in school, we had an assignment asking us to write a poem about how we viewed the world. I searched so many books in the library because I had no idea how I viewed the world. I knew that I thought the world was cold and unfair, but that isn't what they wanted to hear. So, I felt the need to pretend that I was just like everyone else. While in the library that day, though, I found a book on Witchcraft. I took it home and read it thoroughly. *Hey, wait a minute, how come it doesn't say that gay people are an abomination? Why did it say that we are all One? Spells and magic really do exist and the Goddesses have been worshipped for thousands of years?* Oh, it was incredible! I just needed to find out more.

It was a Friday, and I read in that book that under a full moon I could go alone outside, light a candle, and then ask the Goddess for guidance. To be honest, I felt a bit silly, but the questions still burned inside of me. So with a candle and matches in my hand, I headed for the fields behind my house. I walked for about a half an hour with only the light of the moon guiding my way. I picked a spot under a tree and comfortably settled in there.

I looked to the moon as I lit the candle, and asked, "If you are real, make yourself known to me. Answer the questions that I long to know Goddess of the moon; Maiden, Mother, and Crone."

I sat for a long time and nothing happened, but, as soon as I stood up, I felt an amazing sense of kindness toward me. It was a protection that blanketed around me like nothing I had ever felt before. For the first time in my life I felt the acceptance that I had always longed for. I knew right then that Wicca was the path for me! I studied and readied myself over the next couple of weeks and then dedicated myself to the Craft.

When I turned seventeen, I told my family that I was gay and that I was Wiccan. I got the strength from the Goddess. Over time my family has learned to accept that I am gay, but they still won't accept that

I am Wiccan. They are from the generation that will not allow it. They don't talk about it and neither do I, but we have a mutual respect for one another, which is better than nothing.

I'm twenty-eight years old now and I cannot say that I have always followed the path diligently, but one thing I do know is that anytime the road in front of me is dark because I feel that the lessons are too hard to learn or that they just seem so unfair, I can simply light a candle and ask for guidance. The Goddess always answers me in one way or another.

I have learned in life that some lessons must be figured out independently and on our own, and that others are there to bring us back home, but regardless of the reason, I always know that the God and Goddess are there watching over me. They let me know that life never throws you something that you cannot handle. They grant me all that I need and never my selfish wants. I know that they are there; I just feel them all around me. Because of them, I know that I am loved and accepted, which is all I ever truly wanted anyway.

EVERY QUESTION A STEP

by *Taras Stasiuk*

My spiritual path has always been a series of questions.

When I was growing up, we were what my mother called the Once-A-Year People, showing up at the Ukrainian Orthodox church only for Easter, and only for the last half hour, right before the blessing of the food baskets. I wondered about this, and so one year on the way home, I took the first step onto my spiritual path, and asked her the question: "Why *do* we go only once a year?" From this I learned that my mother didn't want to go to church at all, not really, but that it was easier to go once a year than to explain to her own mother why the grandkids didn't go to church. This was an interesting fact for a teenager to absorb: My mother does not want to go to church. Extrapolation: My mother does not feel we *need* to go to church. Conclusion: Either my mother does not fear Hell, or she does not fear Hell as a consequence of absence from church.

Adolescence is the time of testing the world, of pushing personal and societal boundaries, of questioning authority, so this was incredibly exciting: I had an example of one authority figure contradicting another! Mom versus the Orthodox Church, or perhaps, God himself? I had to think about this, hard. I had to ask myself some more very serious questions.

And the only person I could ask was my own self. I knew the church's position, and my mother's. As for the third party involved in this questioning, well, experience had shown that God was going to stay mum on the subject. So I asked myself, "Self, what do *you* think? You've been told all sorts of different things, and now you've discovered that they cannot all be true. Further research has demonstrated great contradiction: there is no person you can turn to for the answers. Except you. So, how do *you* think the Universe works; what cosmic equation makes sense to *you*?"

And that's where all the questioning started, never to end. Since the only person I could rely on for the answers was me, I had to think for myself. This meant research, and always more questions.

There had been hints prior to this that I was the only person who could provide my own answers. I'd already debated with a friend the "What if the *blue* I see is not the same color as what you call *blue*?" question, and I'd decided that since I would never possess the eyeballs of any other person, it didn't matter. My eyeballs saw this blue, so that was my blue, and always would be. In practical terms this question was irrelevant.

On the theoretical side was the Origin of the World debate: Creation or Big Bang? Well, God could have created everything, but what came before God? Did he just show up one day? When he arrived, what was already there for him to arrive *into*? And the Big Bang theory was equally useless to me: There was a bunch of matter that exploded outward. Great. Where did it come from? Did God put it there? It just seemed to me the scientists were replacing God with something different, but not answering any of the questions at all. Once I understood that, I realized that *nobody* knew, so I never would either. As with the profound and impossible question "What happens after death?" I could either flap around helplessly trying to make sense out of insufficient data, or I could accept the unknowing and move on.

From both the practical and theoretical perspective, therefore, I had no answers, except for the ones I decided upon. If God existed, he was obviously not human, and I had to accept that *nobody* would ever have a clear handle on this God being, whatever it was. He might exist, or he might not, and I'd never know. Accept that your blue will always be your blue and deal with it. Accept that you will never know the origin of the Universe, and live your life. With each question, the conclusion was not what was *True*—whatever that means—but what that signified for *me*.

That was my point of view for the next half-decade, until I discovered *The Satanic Bible* by Anton Szandor LaVey. This was the first exposure I'd ever had to someone who not only thought as I did, but then asked the next question: "If there is no God that has any impact on your life, what do you therefore *do* with your life?" I had never considered that question, but it was so obvious in retrospect! In the same way that knowing everything about clockwork doesn't make you a clockmaker until you physically build one, even the most enlightened understanding of the world counts for little until you live according to those precepts. And this is what *The Satanic Bible* is all about. It's a secular humanist handbook, stressing accomplishment in your lifetime and being proud of who you are. God doesn't make the laws; we do. LaVey was expressing a logical extension of my own self-reliance philosophy, and it changed my life.

The Satanic Bible also provided a description of magic from LaVey's point of view. I was initially amazed that someone might think magic without spirituality was possible, and the explanations make for fascinating reading. I'd encountered LaVey's basis while studying psychology among Jung's theories of the collective unconscious, *a priori* knowledge in primates, and the effects of positive thinking in fighting cancer. But while it made sense to me intellectually that magic could work in a world without gods or spiritual energy, I could never fully accept it emotionally. So I did what any responsible self-questioner does, and resolved to study magic a bit more.

Since I'd also studied English literature, among Neo-Pagan magical systems it was Tarot's use of archetype and storytelling that had the most appeal. I studied several decks, and discovered that since the ideas of the Tarot could be extrapolated to any culture and belief system, it was also possible to *learn* about cultures and beliefs by comparing different decks. Like literature and psychology, Tarot was a codification of human experience through selective analogy—a way of explaining the universe.

I tried a reading. It worked. And again I reached a new plateau of understanding: Since Tarot works, magic must work. Eureka!

But then . . . a paradox. I could explain Tarot in nonspiritual terms of the collective unconscious but, like the Big Bang theory, this didn't explain where the collective unconscious itself came from. How did *it* start? Not with the first human surely, since all apes are born with *a priori* aversion to snakes, so where? The primordial soup? Before that?

That's when God tapped me on the shoulder: "Remember when you decided you could never understand me, that nobody ever could? What if *this* is me?" Everything I'd learned, postulated, and deduced came back upon me in a rush: God as energy, prayer healing from a distance, light as energy as particle or wave, humans exhibiting superhuman abilities in times of crisis . . .

And then I saw what LaVey had missed. In his theory of magic he was so focused on the Christian view of God that it never occurred to him that his "scientific" explanations for magic were simply *alternate ways of viewing God*.

I'd already figured out God was unknowable; it was only a short step from there to defining God *as* the unknowable, and any attempt to explain the world—Jungian theory, the Bible, quantum mechanics, fiction, the Tarot—as a way of discussing God. No single means can ever tell the complete story, because simple humans developed all of them, but again, so what? We return to my first spiritual conclusion, the one LaVey reiterated: The only thing I can rely on is what works for me. It's all anyone can rely on.

So I reaccepted the spiritual and stopped self-identifying as a Satanist. I studied Neo-Paganism, meditated, and read Tarot. But I resisted, for a very long time, self-identifying as a Pagan. I didn't want to define myself again without really knowing what that definition entailed. It took another two years.

At a Pagan festival, a few of us performed a simple ritual we'd devised together to make the sun come out. And just before our ritual was finished, the clouds indeed parted. Exultation—and then the inevitable question: Was this *really* the result of our actions, or coincidence? My past experience gave me the answer immediately: I would never know, so it was up to me to decide. And I decided that "Yes, this was *us*." After that, I had to call myself Pagan. I had performed a Pagan ritual, with other Pagans, and it had worked. To deny I was Pagan would be to deny myself.

But what does "Pagan" mean, anyway? I have participated in extensive debates on the topic with many intelligent people, and every single one has reinforced this conclusion: The word Pagan is indefinable. This is hard for many to accept, but what a relief it is to me to know that it doesn't matter! I have accepted that I have no path anyone else can define. Of course they can't—it's *my* path! Every definition of Pagan is as unique as the person holding the definition, and this is the way it should be. I am the only filter through which I can experience God, just as you are the only filter through which you can experience whatever God may be, which we can never know.

Some find this lack of certainty frightening; I find it liberating. It means I can be who I want, choose what I want to do, and be open to every possibility. One day I went from a funk of low self-esteem to having more energy than I'd felt all month, in the space of one creative discussion. This was instructive: Over the course of this half hour, I had been *transformed*. Why? How? If I'm going to question the difficulties of life, I owe it to myself to figure out how to exploit the beauty and the excitement as well!

Which brings me to where I am today. I've studied the questions of what works for me versus what doesn't, from every angle I could think of—intellectual, emotional, spiritual, rational, experiential, hypothetical—and I've made several conclusions. I recognize what makes me happy, and what makes me feel like I'm fulfilling my purpose here on Earth.

All my life, I've had artistic leanings and an interest in people. I have fit these passions into my spiritual path, in a way that is as unique as I am. I've witnessed on innumerable occasions the power of this thing we call Art, which is yet another facet of God. In my spiritual path—in my life path—I use the power of art to remove obstacles, to reveal, to question, to celebrate. An example of this is Tarasmas, my birthday. One of the tenets of Satanism I've retained is the idea that I should celebrate my birthday, since after all it's the most important day of my life. So every Tarasmas I write plays, and have my friends perform them. On that night, everyone remembers how much fun it is to create, and how important it is to play.

What I am here on this planet to do is to inspire people to do what it is *they* are on this planet to do. When I do that, they feel all-powerful, and I have the energy to help the next person in the same way.

Today, I call this path Performance Shamanism. Tomorrow, who knows? I'm keeping an open mind about it.

GRAMMA, I WANT TO BE A WITCH

by Erynn Rowan Laurie

"Gramma, I want to be a witch when I grow up."

It probably wasn't the best way to broach the topic, but I was about twelve or thirteen and had just read an article in the local paper about a coven of witches. What they said and what they did made so much more sense to me than what I learned in church. Unlike some Pagans, my grandmother didn't initiate me into a secret family tradition.

My grandmother, a faithful, very conservative Christian, naturally didn't think much of this witch idea. I got a rather panicked lecture on Satanists and animal sacrifices and the usual anti-Pagan clichés that outsiders hear about us. I dropped the idea at that point, though I still studied astrology and Tarot privately. Back in the mid-1970s, there really wasn't much point in trying to do it any other way; especially given that I lived in rural Western Massachusetts and was significantly underage.

It wasn't until I was twenty-three that I formally became a Pagan. It was a little after I got out of the Navy, and after a two-year stint with the Nichiren Shoshu Buddhists. I never did tell my grandmother that

I had left the Church. I felt it would hurt her too much, given the type of beliefs she held, and I loved her very much and wanted to respect her feelings as best I could under the circumstances. Living an entire continent away made the situation easier on both of us, I suspect. I didn't have to hide my day-to-day life from my family because they simply weren't around to see what I did.

My mom, Bette, has always been the one in my family who has known the most about my spiritual life. When she was out visiting me from her home in New England during my stint as a Buddhist, I took her to a Buddhist meeting. She didn't seem to have any problems with it, despite its strangeness to her. I've always talked fairly openly with her. These days, she reads my LiveJournal to keep up on what I'm doing, and that often includes lengthy posts about my spiritual activities, my theologics, and my involvement with interfaith work and different spiritual communities. She says she's learned more about me through my online writing than she ever has in our conversations over the years.

Mom made my brother and me go to church when we were kids. "Because it's good for you," she told us. "When you're old enough, you can make up your own minds about what you want to do." These days, my brother is an alchemist with a fancy for Thoth. I'm a Celtic Reconstructionist who also follows a number of other non-Christian paths. I'm very thankful for her open attitude about our religious choices.

When I was asked if I'd contribute for this anthology, I wrote an email to my mom and asked if I could interview her about the situation. She kindly agreed and so I sent her some questions about how she felt regarding my Paganism, how she found out, and what her views are about the whole thing. Her answers were honest and forthright, expressing both her uneasiness and her acceptance about my spirituality. I appreciate her honesty more than I can say and I think I understand her a little better because of it.

My mother grew up Protestant. She married a lapsed Catholic in a Catholic ceremony for the sake of harmony in my dad's family. My father, as far as I can tell, is an atheist these days with no interest at all in religion of any kind and a serious antipathy for Catholicism specifically. I know that he was upset when our Irish Catholic neighbors once asked if I'd like to attend mass with them, despite my interest and curiosity. Most of my family was either Polish Catholic or some form of conservative Protestant. My mom's younger brother is a very conservative fundamentalist Christian who runs a children's ministry from a website. He used to do things like pass out Jack Chick tracts on street corners. I attended a nondenominational Protestant church for some years when I was growing up and spent two years attending its private school as well.

When I was first exploring Paganism through eclectic Wicca, my mother was fairly convinced that this was just another phase I was going through. I had, after all, tried a number of Protestant denominations over the years, and had been a Buddhist for a while. None of them had stuck. There was no reason for her to believe that I would remain a Pagan for more than a few years at most. She feels that it's good to know about other religions and the way they change over hundreds or thousands of years and I absolutely agree. Mom has never felt any particular personal need to seek beyond the religion and traditions in which she was raised, however, and I have complete respect for her choices as well.

There are times, she says, when she still thinks perhaps what I do is an escape from some of the things that have happened in my life. I've had my share of difficulties and disappointments, of course. Everyone has challenges they face, and most people find reasons to question the path they follow from time to time. For some, that questioning leads them to return to their path renewed. For others, those questions lead them somewhere entirely new. This was the case for me.

I don't feel, as my mother does, that I left Christianity because its God failed me or abandoned me. When I did believe in the Christianity I was raised in, I was quite serious about it. Yet in exploring other religions, I found that there were different perspectives that often made more sense to me. Asian religions and ancient mythologies drew me strongly, and that newspaper article had sparked something that I could not ignore. Despite my mother's hesitations, she has never felt afraid or panicked about my spiritual explorations. I don't believe she's ever succumbed to the hysteria that has occasionally arisen over accusations of Satanism in Paganism or in any way believes that I worship the Devil. Over the years, she's come to accept both my brother's and my religious and spiritual choices and trusts us to make good decisions for ourselves. She often doesn't really understand what it is we do or why we believe and practice those things, but her acceptance, in and of itself, is a blessing that many other people who become Pagan simply don't get from their families.

Mom admits that she still harbors some hope that my brother and I may someday return to the Christianity we were raised in. I think this is natural for any parent, regardless of the religion they practice. Yet she reads and cheerfully comments on many of my journal entries about my work and she enjoys reading the books and articles I write. I always send her copies of things that I publish and she regards my accomplishment with pride. She even reads them!

My relationship with my mother has always had its ups and downs, yet we've remained close through some very hard times. She's always made an effort to understand me and to try to accept me for who I am, even when it makes her a little uncomfortable. She's been there for me in some very bad situations and has always loved me and supported my decisions, even when she hasn't agreed with them. I've been very blessed and extremely lucky to have her. We don't get to choose our blood families, but we do get to decide how to talk to them, how much to tell them, and how open to be with them about the core of who we are.

Coming out to my family as a Pagan has been a gradual process over the years since I understood that this is where I belonged. At this point I think everyone still living does know, though I realize that some don't particularly approve and may even think it's a little scary or wrong. I've talked to some of the cousins I was closest to growing up, and have never particularly tried to hide my Paganism from anyone except my maternal grandmother. These were not easy decisions and have sometimes required long, deep conversations in order to allay deep-seated fears. In many ways it has been a process of reconciliation with a family that I largely abandoned when I joined the Navy back in 1979, feeling alienated and alone.

We've all changed since that time. There has been a softening of some of the fundamentalism in parts of my family, and more openness on my part to the risks of talking to people whose paths, and sometimes whose actions left me feeling cold or hurt or angry. I can't imagine returning to Christianity, but I can, more and more, see myself as part of my blood family once again. Maybe it's not the years, but the mileage.

Thanks, Mom.

WHILE I WAS SLEEPING

by High Priestess Enoch

To say I came out of the proverbial broom closet doesn't seem to fit me. It was more like being shoved out of it. Well no, that doesn't fit either. I was shoved out of the broom closet and the door locked behind me.

At sixteen years old, hospital machines beeped and whirled around me. Tubes snaked around and into my body. I lay in a coma after a traumatic car accident that resulted in a closed-head injury. For the first weeks, I was in the intensive care unit in the hospital so I could be closely watched. Later, I was moved to a rehabilitation hospital. It was there that I learned how to walk, talk, and eat again after my six-week coma. However, my physical healing is not what was interesting. It is what happened to me spiritually as my body was healing and while I was sleeping.

The world became magical. I was embraced by this magic and I saw other realms, other spirits, and our human spirits. Countless times I detached myself from my physical body to visit other realms and conversed with these friendly entities. I remember doctors, specialists, and nurses presiding over me during the time I was in my coma. I knew what they, and everyone close by, were thinking. If I wanted, I could read what was going to happen to them that day. My tapping into this magical universe did not stop at the hospital, however.

After returning to high school I attempted a normal life. I was changed inwardly and outwardly. I stumbled a lot because of balance problems and spoke painfully slowly. Popularity, gossip, or being the best did not matter to me anymore. Why should it? We were all connected anyhow; magic flowed among us. I still longed to be part of society though, like I was before, and I tried to be, but I remained aloof to many people. I could not relate to their world anymore. So I searched for the magic that I could relate to.

I found friendly fellowship in a Christian church. I enjoyed certain philosophies from the Christian lessons, especially the ones about meditating, creating magic, and about celestial angels. My appetite for this magical information urged me on a search to find faiths specifically centered around this type of information.

So off I went to explore. My first stop was a local group called the Holistic Group. They opened my eyes to the fact that the things that I had experienced in the hospital had names like astral projection, seeing auras, having psychic visions, and visiting other realms. I was able to put things together and reach wonderful epiphanies. It excited me that I found such oneness. I shared it with my close family members who were, for the most part, happy for me. My mom felt it was a good thing for me, and my sister shared many like ideas with me. My dad and stepfather did not really understand it, but never questioned me negatively.

I stayed with the Holistic Group for about five years and I learned about other philosophies that were more open to magic and spiritual entities. I learned about Pagan faiths such as Wicca, Strega, Druidism, and many more. I absorbed them all. While learning about these beliefs, I took the next step involving the world of potent, real magic.

One Day, I ventured into a shop that was advertising for a spiritual healer. The neat little shop had shelves of potions lining its walls. Potions of different types and for different reasons like finding a job, money, luck, or overcoming enemies. While ogling the herb section, I overheard a customer ask the owner of the shop for a psychic reading.

"I'm sorry," he replied in his thick Haitian accent. "The reader is not available today."

I saw a perfect opportunity. I approached the owner and announced my psychic-medium abilities. I gave him my phone number and told him if he needed me to give a reading for a client to contact me. This was one of the most important acts I was to make in my life, as a phone call woke me up one late morning the next week. It was the owner of the shop, Nico.

"Could you give a reading to a client of mine, in about an hour?"

I was excited that he could use my services. I replied, "Yes," and got myself together and headed for the shop. Nico told me ahead of the reading that some clients wanted a Tarot reading because they like to see a visual aid being used. Other clients enjoyed the psychic reading with no tools at all. My first client wanted me to use Tarot cards, which was fine with me because for several years prior, I had studied the Tarot cards. In that time I learned that the Tarot cards were used to form a doorway into the subconscious. I also learned why traditional organized religions are against this whole concept, so of course, that made me want to learn more! So, needless to say, I learned to read the Tarot very well. As the years went on, I developed a system using just my abilities followed up with a quick Tarot showing. Later, Nico gave me my own office to give readings. I enjoyed reading Nico's clients for seven years. I did thousands of readings during that time, which boosted my psychic ability to the height that it was when I was in the hospital. I also learned that Nico was a very sought after spiritual healer and a respected practitioner of the magic known as a Santero.

During this time I had been anointed as a Wiccan priestess and a Druid. I was drawn to the Druid faith, especially, because Druids were into everything. A Druid was expected to know about divination, mediumship, herbs, magic, quantum physics, aliens, and archangels, which were all perfect for my endless study of the mystical and magical. Later on, I got lucky because I found a Druid circle—Bethany Coven of the Oak—that offered Wiccan ceremonies as well! The Elder of that circle was also a Christian. Everything fit. It was in that circle that I was ordained as a Druid and a Wiccan High Priestess. However, I chose not to tell all of my Christian family the news because I did not want to have to explain my simultaneous love for Christianity, Druidism, and Wicca.

I moved to another city and had to leave Nico. I was excited to move somewhere new, but at the same time, sad to leave all of the friends I'd met. After all, they represented monumental steps I made spiritually and magically. Of course, I knew that I would find new opportunities, but letting go of the old was hard.

When in the new city, I joined a chapter of the national Covenant for United Universal Pagans (CUUPS). I also started my own coven and study group called the Mystics, which is still running today, something I am proud of. I love sharing new information on magic, spirituality, and philosophies with others. I see the beautiful opportunity to aid other people evolving in their faith, whether Pagan, magical, or just plain spiritual. I also started my own website which offers my abilities to the public.

Throughout the years, I have found people are confused about my love for both Christianity and Paganism. I tell them what was revealed to me while I lay sleeping in the hospital. The All, whether perceived as a God, or a Goddess, or as one being, or even as an energy field, cares only about one thing: Love. Absolute and unconditional love.

TURNING

by Jessica Jenkins

I grew up in a suburban area surrounded by large plots of land abundant with wildlife. My family believed it was very important for my brother and me to spend as much time outside as possible. I remember dancing in the rain as it pummeled the ground, and racing through our yard as the sun warmed the earth and the verdant gardens. I remember exploring rocks that were covered with moss and had centipedes hiding underneath. I remember how we would turn off all the lights and watch while the earth trembled as thunderstorms flashed and tore through the sycamore trees. In the summer I would help in the garden, stealing herbs and rose petals to leave in decorative patterns with sticks and rocks in the soft grass or hidden in a crook of a tree branch. I did not know exactly what I was doing, only that it felt right and incredibly beautiful. I truly believe that my spirituality is rooted in nature and in being at peace with myself.

My family attended a small Anglican church. I don't remember the precise lessons we were taught in Sunday school, but I do remember learning friendship, caring and generosity. As I grew older I never understood why we had to go to church if God made the earth. Wasn't he all around? Didn't he know what was in my heart when I was outside of the church? Wasn't God able to listen to our prayers at home? So why did I need to go to a church for him to really hear me, or for him to know my intentions? I was very confused and I voiced my opinions. As we grew older, slowly my mum gave my brother and me the ability to decide for ourselves: Would we like to go to church or would we like to stay home? Like any eight year old, I voiced that I'd rather be outside playing and rushed out to join the other neighborhood children.

During my teenage years religion and spirituality were not at the forefront of my mind. At least, they weren't until one day a friend showed up wearing a five-pointed star and carrying a book entitled *To Ride a Silver Broomstick*. I was so curious. With a small group of close friends, I spent hours talking about spellcasting, tarot cards, herbal properties, and gods and goddesses. I had never even considered that a deity could be female, and I relished the idea. However, I was uncomfortable with how the other students saw my friend. They started to point at her in the hallways and call her a witch, taunting her to put spells on them and generally trying their best to point out everything that made her different. I was torn. Wasn't being a witch bad? Didn't they put small children in ovens and fly through the air? Weren't they very ugly? I understood why the high school children rebelled against her, but I also saw her wearing her pentacle every day, rooted in her faith. As a group we kept to ourselves and tuned out the general population. I did not really consider myself to be a witch or Pagan at the time, but in the years to come I would find myself calling on the Goddess when I was scared or in need of guidance.

Many years passed and we all went our separate ways. I moved far away to the city to live on my own while going to university. It was a huge change. I was working almost full time while trying to complete a full time double major at university. After a few semesters of working, and working, and working, I felt very hollow. Very lonely. Very . . . incomplete. I was so sad. I just remember these days as permanently grey: The tall buildings, the rushing, the necessity of appearing happy and to please the people at work, the customers, the people from school, the amount of homework and papers. I felt very fake and wondered if I was ever going to enjoy life again. I longed for my heart to sing and my spirit to feel at peace.

During this time I discovered that my biological grandparents had passed away a few years before. I felt guilty that I never got to spend time with them, to tell them just how much I thought about them, how much I had loved them even though we had not been able to spend time together. I decided then and there I would not lose any more of myself, and I began to research the origins of my families, and their history. I knew my grandparents had been Welsh, so I began researching that culture, spending many evenings learning Welsh customs and even a little of the language. Eventually I began to read about religion in Wales, including Pagan customs. That word threw me back to my high school years, and more importantly, how I had felt when I had been with the group of like-minded girls: strong, independent, and simply enough, happy.

Set upon this new path, I began looking up Paganism once again, and came across the web page for the Crescent Moon School. Taking courses through this school was one of the major pivot points in my life. I learned about celebrating the Sabbats through ritual, about energy work (which came surprising easily and quickly), about herbalism, divination, the different paths of paganism and so very, very much about myself. I felt at ease in my new studies. I also met one of my dearest spiritual partners at this school. As we progressed through the levels, we designed new rituals for the school, and then for the public. I loved giving back to the community that had so warmly welcomed me when I had begun my own spiritual path. A few years into my new spiritual leanings, I was invited to join a private coven associated with the Black Forest Circle and Seminary. When I found out they were training people to become clergy I felt that my calling to the Pagan community had come full circle. I was now able to offer people more then just a spiritually fulfilling ritual; I could provide a wealth of information, spiritual counseling, and services such as ritual design, handfastings, Wiccanings, and crossing over rites.

One of the main challenges that I faced was sharing my religion with my family. It saddens my heart that my spirituality makes me feel so complete, but it unnerves them. I have tried on more then one occasion to express that I do believe in the concept of "God," or the gods and goddesses of mythology (who in my opinion make up a greater whole than we could ever conceive of), but to very little avail. However, I have come to the realization that as long as my spirituality makes me happy, I do not need to justify it to everyone, or shout it out from the rooftops. My spirituality is very personal, and not many people outside of the Pagan community even know. Which, considering the preconceptions people have about Wiccans, leaves me more peace of mind. Of course, when people ask me a direct question about my religious beliefs, I answer that I am Wiccan, and if they do not know what that means, I explain that in its simplest form, it is a religion based on natural cycles and seasons, and that I find it spiritually fulfilling.

When my Pagan fiancé and I became engaged, we faced another challenge concerning our families: planning a wedding. We are both comfortable in our religion and beliefs, but not everyone in our families is. We wanted to celebrate this occasion with our families present, while being true to our spirituality. We were torn. Should we have a traditional handfasting? How many people would be uncomfortable with this, and should we care if they were? My gut reaction was that I did care: I did not want to invite people to a ceremony where they would be uncomfortable. I would not be comfortable if they weren't, therefore if we wanted our families at the ceremony, it was going to have to feel safe and somewhat familiar to them. We are lucky that a large part of both our families are Scottish. We decided to go back to our roots and honor them with a Scottish wedding. We are having a minister officiate, although he is not associated with a specific church; instead, he fills the role of a spiritual counselor at a local children's hospital, something I admire greatly, partly due to my love of children, but also because of his comfort handling all the religions he interacts with on a daily basis. We asked if he would be comfortable providing a nondenominational spiritual ceremony, and luckily he was not only comfortable but also very open to different religious customs. We are able to have the handfasting ceremony included in our ritual while we recite our vows; there will be a unity candle; the altar will be set with remembrance roses for those who have passed on; and we will have traditional readings from other religions instead of the Christian Bible. One special tradition that I would never have discovered if we had not researched our Scottish roots is a beautiful ceremony performed after the wedding called the pinning of the plaid, where my new husband's family welcomes me by giving me a gift of a sash made of their family tartan, pinned to my gown by my mother-in-law. Our willingness to accommodate our families has allowed us to incorporate many spiritual traditions into our wedding without making anyone uncomfortable, and especially without making us feel as if we had to leave our spirituality behind to appease others.

One part of my spirituality that I feel very strongly about is that you need to "walk the talk," and so I try to incorporate the philosophies that I support in during my daily life. That meant I wanted a job that would allow me to be outside for much of the day, and that I would enjoy and look forward to every day. I love working with children, and that lead me to completing a degree in Early Childhood Education. The daycare where I work is extremely multicultural, and I find the differences in language, backgrounds, and religions fascinating. Our daycare was originally Christian, and is still associated with one of the churches. Many of the people I work with are devoted Christians. I do not flaunt my religion, but I don't hide it, either. I do wear my pentacle and if they ask me about it I explain that each point represents the elements and my spirit. Some of my co-workers were interested in hearing more; however, the majority of people find the straightforward answer sufficient.

One way I try to practice my spirituality every day at work is by spending time outside. My class and I go out every day, no matter what the weather. I pass along my love of nature to them by saving worms from rainy sidewalks, and showing them how ants build their homes. We study whatever the children are interested in, and part of me is always surprised by how drawn they are to nature, growth, cycles, and seasons. One of the hardest challenges I faced was working in the downtown core of the city. What little green space there is can at times be covered in garbage. But there is beauty, too: We have explored different parks, green spaces, outdoor pools and beautiful hidden gardens that are tucked away neatly from most of the public. Nature is indeed all around, even in the city, where the cement can feel overwhelming.

When people come to me with life challenges, the one piece of advice I always give is from the Charge of the Goddess: "If that which you seek, you find not within yourself, you will never find it without." Knowing yourself is the first step to spiritual fulfillment that you will not find in gods, goddesses, spells or rituals. Each of us knows the answers to our deepest questions, the truth or purpose of our lives. Each one of us, whether we are Christian, Muslim, Buddhist, or Wiccan is a High Priest and High Priestess that is waiting to be found. Spirituality is not something one can grab in the outside world; it comes from within.

A Name for What I Am

by Tracey Costa

When asked when I became Wiccan, I smile and say, "I was just born this way." It was never a question of whether or not I became Wiccan, for me, it was not having any idea that there was actually a name out there for who and what I was.

From the time I was very young, I can remember many things that I would say or do that seemed to fall right in line with being Wiccan. Even when my friends dared one another to stand on Witch's Rock, a huge rock with a hole we called a witch eye, I was first in line to stand on it. So many kids were afraid of Witch's Rock, but I was the only one who wasn't afraid; I actually thought it was cool. It was there that I started my rock and crystal collection.

I was raised Catholic, but when I would pray, I prayed to a Woman of the Universe. I didn't know exactly how to label her, so I called her Mary, Mother of Jesus. She was the only one I wanted or felt comfortable praying to. I believed that she was the Goddess. When I prayed to her I felt the presence of angels all around me and was gifted enough to always experience visions.

As I got older, I never actually practiced Christianity. I had no interest in the religion, nor did I have anything vested in it. I had my own beliefs, and just knew that as much as what comes around goes around, the moon has a mystical and unexplainable power. This all seemed so natural to me that I never gave it a second thought. I was just going about my life and enjoying worship on my own.

One day, my husband saw a program on television about alternative modern spiritual paths, focusing on Wicca. He called to me from the other room and said, "Hey, look at this, these people are just like you!" I watched in amazement. There actually was a name for the way I had always lived, a name for what I believed in! I couldn't believe that there were other people out there like me, people who were open. I wanted to be proud like them, too.

Shortly after seeing her on television, I contacted the leader of the Wiccan group—I just had to learn what it was all about. I was scared though, because I had never heard of Wicca before in my life, and I really didn't know anyone who was Wiccan. The High Priestess and I spoke several times on the phone and she helped me through some really tough times, but, although I lived only a little over an hour away, I just wasn't ready to make the trip to visit her and her group. I was not feeling well at that time and was told by my doctors that I needed a major surgery. I was really scared and spoke to the High Priestess before I was admitted to the hospital. She made me feel better and I knew that God and Goddess were pulling for me.

The morning of my surgery, as I was being put under anesthesia, something went terribly wrong. My lung collapsed and I almost didn't make it. They couldn't do the surgery that day and had to reschedule it. As soon as I got home from the hospital, I called the High Priestess in a complete panic. I thought the craziest thoughts, but I couldn't help it. I thought that because I was given time off from work and the surgery was rescheduled to another week, that this was my chance to bond with my children and my husband for the last time before I would die in surgery. She quickly talked me out of that nonsense and supported me through the week before the surgery, all the while helping me find trust and inner peace in the God and Goddess. After the week went by, I had my surgery and everything went perfectly, but I was in the hospital feeling alone and sick. To my amazement, the High Priestess came to see me. I looked at her and said, "Okay, I know I am on painkillers, but have I died?" We laughed together and I knew I was going to be okay after my first blessing from her. I could feel the presence of the God and Goddess around me.

I have since attended services with that Wiccan group. I feel like I finally found where I belong and that is a huge blessing. The more I read and learn about Wicca, the more I confirm that this is how I was born. I feel complete and I am so happy that I can finally pray to the God and Goddess in a place of worship. The Wiccan group is always so warm and welcoming and, to top it off, I feel like I have known the High Priestess in past lives.

I told my mother all about my newfound faith and church. From these conversations, I have learned that she felt there was a natural Witch inside of her too. We have talked a lot about Wicca and she is very supportive even though my father is not crazy about it. My husband and children accept Wicca and are very supportive, especially my daughter, who was also born with natural gifts. I can't even begin to say how happy I am for her that she, too, has found a name for how she feels. She no longer wonders why we are the only ones.

THE SHIFTING TIDES OF FAITH

by Ceri Young

It's hard to reconcile where I am now with where I was when I first got interested in Paganism. My practice has changed so much over the years that it doesn't resemble anything like what I did when I first started. Even saying when exactly I first started is kind of murky.

I used to tell people that I came to Wicca after watching the movie *The Craft*. For those who don't remember it, it was a 1996 film that followed a group of four girls who perform magic rituals, hoping to gain real power. They discover that magic is real (albeit *Hollywood* real), and most of them then get drunk on their own power. Chaos ensues.

It wasn't a great movie, but something about it captivated me. While I didn't have any designs on finding a magic spell that would teach me how to fly, there was something about the rituals depicted that I found really compelling. I made the connection between the movie and Wicca—which someone had mentioned to me at a party a few months before—and I started doing research.

I searched the web. I distinctly remember my first search on Wicca turned up thirteen results; this was in the days before Google. Mostly what I found were answers to common questions and recommendations for books. I made a list of suggested reading. At the top of my list at the time were *Drawing Down the Moon* by Margot Adler and *The Spiral Dance* by Starhawk.

Local stores didn't carry a whole lot of Paganism-related books, so one afternoon my best friend and I combed downtown Halifax, determined to check every used and new bookstore to see if we could find something. There are a lot of bookstores in downtown Halifax, and at the end of the day we were pretty tired, which is how we ended up walking right by Halifax's local Pagan bookstore, Little Mysteries, without stepping inside. We didn't realize our mistake until many weeks later! I ended up making a special order for the books I wanted.

I read a lot, and I thought a lot (and probably to the chagrin of my friends, I talked a lot about what I was reading, I can only imagine how boring I must've been). I tried the basic exercises in *The Spiral Dance*. I did my term documentary for journalism school on Pagan weddings. I tried some rituals myself, but I just felt silly. Eventually, I shelved my books.

My parents thought I had gone through a weird phase and grown out of it. They were right about it being a phase, but I hadn't grown out of Paganism. I was still growing *into* it. I wasn't yet ready to take a step and declare myself Wiccan, but it was always there, at the back of my mind. And the more I thought about it, the more I realized that I had been moving slowly in that direction all along.

In fact, long before I ever saw *The Craft*, a friend loaned me the *Clan of the Cave Bear* series of books by Jean M. Auel. The books are set in prehistoric times, and most of the characters worship a Mother goddess who birthed the world. I was raised Catholic, so I had the concept of a male creator god lodged pretty firmly in my brain. Imagining creation coming from a Goddess completely shifted my world view. I remember calling my friend on the phone and enthusing about it. She was completely uninterested, but it made so much more sense to me.

I would call it a turning point in my spiritual life, and I suppose it was, except at the time I had no idea that there might be people who still worshipped a Goddess rather than a God, or that I could take up doing the same thing. I suppose it goes to show what a sheltered life I led that the idea didn't even occur to me.

These turning points go back even farther than that. In my early teens, I owned a book called *The Moons of Madeleine* by Joan Clark. The book is a coming-of-age story about a girl named Madeleine. While looking through a hand-carved moon mask, Madeleine sees a girl of about her own age in the back yard. The girl is wearing a white toga, and is part of a group of moon priestesses: girls who all look alike, and whose faces reflect the phases of the moon. Madeleine is asked to help them solve a dispute among the priestesses by finding two egg-shaped stones that were hidden in her world. I won't say the book was one of my favorites, but the imagery definitely stuck with me over the years. Looking back now, the connections to Greek mythology and Goddess worship are pretty obvious, but I didn't know anything about it at the time.

I suppose this is what people mean when they say that finding Paganism feels like coming home. There is the big moment when you find out about Paganism, and it feels like something you've known all along but didn't have words for. For me, this was because Paganism (and Wicca in particular, which is what I was first drawn to) grouped together a lot of little things that had interested me all along. It was the missing piece to a puzzle I didn't know I'd been putting together.

But I still wasn't ready yet. Even after finding out that there were Pagan faiths, I still wasn't convinced that it was a path for me. I moved from Halifax to Montreal, and my books came with me. Eventually I went back to them. I was ready to try ritual again. I took Wicca 101 courses from a local group, and went to local events and rituals. I joined some online mailing lists. Eventually, I was involved with setting up the Montreal Pagan Resource Centre, which offers people a space to read books related to Pagan topics.

My practice has wandered around a lot. I didn't join a coven right away, since I was more interested in figuring out what I wanted to do and finding a group that matched my goals. Since then, I've been involved in two ongoing groups (one informal study group, and one coven) and I enjoyed the energy and excitement of working with good friends toward common goals. I currently work alone, and enjoy the freedom and lack of structure. For me, Paganism is a path that matches everything else in my life—no rigid structure lasts for long. Eventually I'll shift away from something, maybe to come back to it months or years later with a fresh perspective, ready to try again. I'll be interested in Tarot almost exclusively for a while, then switch to labyrinth meditations. I'll read up about folk practice or mythology for a while; then put what I've been learning into ritual. My current practice is based around my home and kitchen—working magic into the food I cook. My beliefs change, and my understanding changes as I go. It's much like my first years of taking my books off the shelf and putting them back again. The difference is that now I definitely apply the term Pagan to what I am. What variety of Pagan depends on when you happen to ask me.

My parents still think I'm a little odd for wanting to follow this path, but they don't object. My mother asks me lots of questions about what I believe and what I do. I think she might be a little confused by how much my practice changes from year to year. My extended family occasionally raises an eyebrow when I mention things like *ritual* and *coven*, but that's it. My mother-in-law has no end of fun telling people that "My daughter-in-law is a real witch,"—sometimes while I'm in the room—to see how they react.

After ten years of study and about eight years of practice, my faith is still surprising me. I don't know where it will go after this, but I am enjoying going with the flow.

OUR STORIES ARE THE SAME

by Gregory Michael Brewer

Split the veil and burn the fires!

Sorry, just wanted your attention. Now that I have it, help me out here! How do you think this story should begin? *The Burning Times are over?* No, we know that's not really true. *I was raised a Christian, but I always knew I was a Witch?* That's kind of boring. *The moon was full, the wind was blowing, and for the first time nature whispered its secret mystery?* I could use imagery and craft beautiful sentences, but I don't think that's going to work either. Why not? Well, you already know.

We are kith and kin. We have different stories, different backgrounds, and different views. But the story is really the same. We are witches.

So here is my story, and may it bless you.

As a boy I was curious about everything. In the school library I found a book about palmistry and checked it out. My father told me it was "of the occult" and instructed me to return it. So I did. I learned quickly not to speak of such things.

In time, I gave my heart to Jesus; everyone was doing it. But I still wanted to read those occult books. My curiosity wasn't stifled.

At nineteen, I was confused and living on my own for the first time. And like so many others, I just wasn't satisfied with my religious upbringing. It didn't work for me and I found no place for it in my life. And living on my own meant I could do whatever I wanted so long as my parents didn't find out.

In the summer of 1992 I was working as a third-shift cook. Working in a twenty-four hour food service business, you never knew who would be walking in and you got used to meeting quite a variety of folks.

When Jonathon walked in, I thought nothing of it. He was just another customer. I had no idea that he was to become one of my best friends and my future teacher. Business was slow that night, and as he sat at his table he began giving Tarot card readings to the other customers. I was fascinated. Eventually, I made my way to his table and he did a reading for me. What he revealed was so accurate that I was amazed, and wanted to learn more. He agreed to teach me and we started meeting on a regular basis outside of work. In time, I told him that I was really interested in Witchcraft, and he said that he could teach me that also.

He did not follow the Wiccan faith, but was instead a self-proclaimed Witch, meaning that he knew how to cast spells and direct energy in order to manifest desired results. In fact, I had no idea what Wicca was at that time, only Witchcraft: power, spells, and magic. It was exactly what I wanted! With persistence and diligence I worked under his instruction. I got what I asked for and then some.

Eventually we parted company, but I continued to study and practice on my own. However, in time I realized that I was in this for all the wrong reasons: selfish motives, power, and greed. Once I realized this, I burned my books and turned away from the Craft altogether.

It wasn't long before I found myself sitting in church again and rededicating my heart to Jesus. I had to experience Christianity by my own choosing, not because it was what I was taught. But again I began to feel the tug of misery, stronger than ever. I did find Jesus, truly, but His religion didn't work for me. I felt like a prisoner, and I was. I knew I was a Witch.

Because of this battle back and forth, it seemed like so much time passed for me without having any religion or spirituality. I had to find myself. But life is a circle, a mystery, and all things eventually return to their source. One night I really did step outside when the moon was shining and the wind was blowing, but I had grown up. That's when I felt it. I will never forget that night, and I will never forget that voice. It was like my mother, like my grandmother, but different and greater. I felt the energy of the sky, the earth, the wind, and the All. And it did whisper a mystery.

She said, "Now you are ready!"

That night I felt happiness, I felt freedom, and I felt true spirituality for the first time. But even then it was a struggle. I had to learn that I knew nothing. I also had to learn that it was okay to think for myself and that my happiness, my true salvation, was not dependent on the approval of others.

I dedicated myself to the God and Goddess, and to the Old Ways. But there was still Mom and Dad. They were my parents, and don't we all want our parents' approval? Don't we need it? Although it wasn't easy, I decided that they were going to have to accept me for the complete person I was. I would accept nothing less. Nothing ever made me happier than when I left Christianity, although it is a beautiful religion. It just wasn't for me. Mom and Dad were going to accept this, just as I accepted them.

I can tell you that I knew my parents were always going to be my parents and I would always be their son, no matter what. Mom and Dad are still Christian, but they are still Mom and Dad. We are kith and kin; we are blood. They don't judge me, but instead accept me for who I am: their son.

That was a long time ago and since then I've learned, studied, practiced, and have been initiated into the third degree. I now oversee a Wiccan study group, and am happier than I've ever been in my life.

As Wiccans, we live and let live. We fairly take and fairly give. So ride your broomsticks, chant your spells, and let yourselves be happy. Know that you are complete and loved. In time you will learn that there is no need for spells anymore, because the only world you need to change is yours!

FACING PREJUDICE WITHIN

by Cerridwen Johnson

Unlike most Wiccans, I was born into the religion. My father is Gardnerian, so I grew up in a traditional coven in the United States. I can honestly say that most of the time I felt like it was the greatest way to grow up. I not only had two parents caring for me, but also a whole coven of family looking out for me. On the other hand, when I got into trouble, I didn't just have two parents that were disappointed in me, but instead a whole coven family that was disappointed in me. That certainly was a heavy load to carry! But over all, it was great.

I was more of a Sabbat Wiccan. My religion wasn't an all encompassing part of my life, and like most kids, I rebelled in my teen years. I just didn't want to do what my family was doing anymore, so I started seeking a different spiritual path. I looked into Buddhism, Hinduism, and many others. My parents joke to this day that when I rebelled, I never went monotheistic. By the time I was eighteen, I had decided that yes, I actually did want to be a Gardnerian. Part of me wanted to follow this path because it's how I was raised, but mostly, I wanted to follow it because of how it spoke to my heart. Up until then, my parents and coven family kept me pretty well sheltered. I mean, I knew that there was prejudice, but until I started practicing as an *official* Gardnerian I really just had no idea. Who would have ever thought that a community of eclectic Wiccans and Pagans, who themselves face bigotry in their daily lives, could then turn around and treat me the same way? I was a *liberal* Gardnerian, so I also faced harassment from the more fundamentalist or hardcore community. I can't even tell you the number of times that I would show up at a Pagan gathering and hear, "Oh, she's Gardnerian. Just ignore her." I never even had a chance to introduce myself! And on the few occasions where people did not know who I was and I actually could introduce myself, they often went from being nice and polite to rude and mean when they found out about my family's Gardnerian path.

I am now twenty-five, a first degree initiate, and a Peace Corps volunteer in Africa. I live in a small Muslim village in the middle of the bush. It takes me two days to travel for an Internet connection, or even electricity, where I am happy to e-mail my family and friends. But I feel more comfortable as a Gardnerian in my village than I do in America! I was asked by the Imam, "Do you believe in God?" My nervous response was, "Well, yes, but not the Muslim one." And do you know what they said? "That's okay. All that matters is that you believe in some God." That's more acceptance than I have gotten in the Pagan community in America! So much for America and freedom of religion.

So many Wiccans I have met think the gods are archetypes, and so few truly believe. Maybe that's because so many of the Wiccan books out there are ninety percent ritual magic and only ten percent beliefs.

So many Pagans don't even realize that Wicca is a religion and that it's not just a set of practices. We all know that there is something out there bigger than us when we are kids, but somewhere along the way, we lose that knowing. And to everyone's detriment, many of the people in this world never find it again. Well, I wanted to find it again, so my freshman year of college I decided to do a self-dedication. It was nothing fancy. I was an adult and I knew what I wanted. I did it on October 31. Looking back, it's actually a little embarrassing. I screwed up. Everything I did was wrong. I chalked my ritual circle, and you would have sworn I was taking acid by looking at it; I was that nervous. I wonder now why I was so scared and anxious. Why did I think it was so important that everything had to be perfect? It didn't matter. I drew the circle and called the Watchtowers. Part of me wanted to quit right then and there, but I didn't. I just kept going and invoked the gods. In that moment, I may have lost the wonder of childhood, but I was given something different, something so much better. The only way I can describe it is by the feeling I got in the pit of my stomach; you know, the one that tells you that you're not alone? You just know everything is going to be okay and that the gods are with you. Well, that's exactly what happened to me. But the most interesting part of the story is that I didn't tell anyone what I was planning. The next day, I called my dad and told him all about it. It turns out that I did my self-dedication thirty years to the day after he did his. I guess that's when I knew beyond a shadow of a doubt that I was where I was supposed to be, and that I was doing what I was supposed to do. Since then, I have never looked back.

IF ONLY I HAD KNOWN ABOUT
THE BROOM CLOSET . . .

by Junior Crone

I cannot claim that I ever came out of the broom closet, because I didn't even know that I had the option of hiding in said closet when I began to self-identify as a Pagan at the age of seventeen. I also never truly felt the need to hide my spiritual self-expression, since the gods saw to it that at an early age my peers would be aware of my difference thanks to the path my life had taken.

Don't get me wrong. I realize how fortunate I am to have been born in a culture in which I could explore my spirituality and contribute to the academic study of Paganism without ending up in a straightjacket. I was born in Quebec in 1979, almost two decades after the Quiet Revolution began. Like many young Québécois of my generation, I grew up in a social and cultural environment that had all but purged itself of the influence of the Roman Catholic Church, which had been nearly all-powerful within the province until the 1960s.

My parents were among those who had left the Church *en masse* and never looked back. My father—who had been given a strict private

84

education in a *collège classique* run by priests (as was the norm at the time)—had a particularly contemptuous opinion of the Roman Catholic religion. His chosen profession as a medical doctor reinforced his dismissal of a belief system that would have people accept the literal truth of the Resurrection, or even the Virgin Birth. My mother, on the other hand, had been given only minimal religious instruction while growing up in her native Portugal, which she left in the 1960s to look for better opportunities than those that were offered to young women under the fascist Salazar regime of the time.

Neither of my parents wanted their children to be raised with any kind of religious instruction, so my siblings and I were spared a Roman Catholic upbringing. My father would often claim that we were pagans (*païens*), in the Québécois colloquial sense of being irreligious, whenever we asked him which religion we followed.

In spite of my secular upbringing, my parents were known to hold Solstice parties every year at midsummer, my father always seemed to know when the next full moon would occur, and always seemed eager to celebrate Christmas a few days before December 25. Also, I became aware early in life that there was more within nature than a mechanistic view of the world would have anyone believe. As a child I thought that animals and trees had a spirit about them. Having spent most of my first six years living in the picturesque town of Mont-Saint-Hilaire (known for its apple orchards and for being a bedroom community to nearby Montreal), I would sometimes feel myself surrounded by such entities while playing among the dozen apple trees in our yard, or in the many wooded areas and parks on the mountain.

In 1985, my family moved south of the border. During the six-odd months we lived in southern Florida, my imaginary spirit-friends came to include the sea creatures that dwelled in the nearby Atlantic. The following year, after returning to Mont-Saint-Hilaire, my family began a residential pattern in which we moved and I changed schools every year. This pattern lasted until 1991, when I started the eighth grade. In the fall of 1987, my family moved to Portugal. I loathed my new surroundings, and grew increasingly uneasy about the unwanted intrusion of Roman Catholicism in my environment. I became rather disgusted with what I interpreted then as the extreme hypocrisy within the religion. I also missed Canada terribly and longed to be home and away from the strange land to which I had been spirited away. As a psychological defense mechanism I developed the notion that only *bad* or inexcusably backward or ignorant people worshipped the Christian God, so it stood to my unsophisticated, eight-year-old logic that *good* and clever people worshipped the-opposite-of God. Back then, just being aware of how subversive such thoughts truly were brought me immense satisfaction—if not joy. Of course, I told no one about my childlike heresy.

My rudimentary flirtation with the left-hand path was short-lived. I grew out of it almost as soon as my family moved back to Canada by the end of the school year. Still, I learned an important lesson in the power of subversive and marginal thought, if only that thinking subversively could carry me through dark times until things improved.

To my horror and disappointment, we returned to Portugal in 1990. My second stay in my mother's native land caused me not to rediscover devils or monsters, but to become acquainted with the gods of ancient Greece and Rome.

Learning about ancient myths and beliefs was part of the history curriculum for my grade at my *lycée*. First I learned about Egyptian mythology, and then we quickly moved on to the Greek myths. I remember learning about the Olympian gods at the same time, although Hera caught my attention the most. In hindsight, although I did not identify as Pagan back then, I can trace my first experience of the goddess to reading my history book and being inexplicably drawn to Her name when I was eleven years old. I immersed myself in Greek mythology, read parts of the *Illiad*, and this time I did not keep my new passion a secret from anyone. My keen interest in my favorite Goddess survived my family's return to Canada in the summer of 1991.

By that time, my life experiences and travels had created a huge gap between my classmates and myself. There was very little common ground to be had, and my constant changing of schools every year caused me to unwittingly skip a grade. So I found myself to be the only trilingual twelve-year-old eighth-grader in my class, and possibly in my entire junior high school. I was known as hopelessly different and odd, and in the ninth grade I became known as the resident Classical mythology geek. I stood out so much that some of my classmates suspected me of being a federalist, which came as close to a mortal sin in the post–Quiet-Revolution Quebec of the early-to-mid 1990s as anything ever could, mainly because I was one of the very few people at school (including the English teachers) who was perfectly fluent in English, and therefore had less reason to want Quebec to separate from Canada and become its own independent country.

I graduated from my *polyvalente* at age sixteen, and in the following years, while studying at the local CEGEP, I discovered the existence of Paganism in Montreal through sheer dumb luck.

In 1997, my brothers were both attending McGill University and sharing an apartment in downtown Montreal, one block away from the location of the well-known occult store *Le Mélange Magique* (in English, The Magical Blend, or simply the Mélange as it's known in the bilingual city). On the day my brothers, some of our friends, and I made an expedition to the city to see the theatrical re-release of the original *Star Wars: Episode IV* movie, we made a quick stop at the Mélange before the show. By then I had heard some whispers about Wicca, and all that I really knew at the time was that some people considered witchcraft to be a religion based on observing the cycles of nature. Truth be told, I knew little else about Pagan witchcraft than what I had seen in the movie *The Craft*, which had been released the previous year. Yet the notion that a religion of Pagan witchcraft existed in the real world had always intrigued me, and I yearned to know more.

The Mélange was my first real introduction to Wicca and Paganism, and to the Pagan community in Montreal. It was through the Montreal Pagan newsletter *8Sabbats* that I found the number of a networking resource person, whom I called one fateful evening to find out what I could about Paganism and how I could meet Pagans in my favorite city in the entire world. The person told me about the Concordia University Pagan Society (CUPS) and their biweekly Bardic evenings, during which people would come and share songs and stories that related to all things Pagan. I decided that I would go to the next meeting, which was to be held the following Wednesday. All that was left for me to do was to convince my mother to let me borrow the car to go to Montreal by myself on a school night to visit a bunch of Pagan strangers for no other discernible reason than sheer curiosity.

At first, my parents were quite shocked and concerned about my newfound interest in Paganism. Although they had thus far accepted my interest in mythology without asking too many questions, this time they were afraid that I was about to join a cult, and would not let me go to the Bardic meeting without one of my older brothers present. Fortunately for me, they selected my middle brother for the task, who was only two years older than I and whom I was able to convince that I was much too stubborn and aggravating to be successfully brainwashed in any way. I reminded him of how long I had been interested in mythology (a passion I still maintained several years after returning from that second trip to Portugal), and nature religion. My brother was the first person I told of my experience of nature spirits in our old home on the Mont-Saint-Hilaire, and of my dabbling with subversive paradigms during our first stay in Portugal.

He was quite impressed with the extent of my sophistication in all things esoteric and otherworldly, especially considering that he had been given the same Agnostic upbringing as I had, and yet he had none of the curiosity about Pagan gods and nature spirits that I always seemed to possess. He quickly convinced my mother to let me go unaccompanied to the CUPS Bardic evening.

My first contact with Montreal Pagans outside of the Mélange was interesting, although the members of CUPS, most of whom were Concordia University students, were wary of me because they found that I was a little too young to be attending their events (I was two weeks shy of my eighteenth birthday on that first visit to the CUPS Bardic). Nonetheless, I began attending the Bardic evenings on a more regular basis after reaching the age of majority, and my parents had no choice but to become accustomed to my latest eccentricity. It took no time at all to convince my best friend to accompany me to the public Sabbats held in Montreal, as she was as interested in nature religion and Pagan witchcraft as I had always been. I am still amazed at the astronomical odds of having a friend like her at the time. We are friends to this day, though I doubt that she identifies as a Pagan anymore.

By the time I moved to Montreal to pursue my studies in anthropology at Concordia University in the fall of 1998, most of my friends were local Pagans, and to my great surprise, I became better acquainted with a relative who also happened to be a witch. I had known that there was at least one female relative on my father's side of the family who was into occult pursuits, but I hadn't known that there were others as well. Perhaps this explains my parents' resignation about my newfound spirituality of choice. A few years after I had acquired a Pagan identity, my father admitted to me that he would have liked to have studied anthropology and to have been a Pagan when he was my age.

So much for hiding in the broom closet!

WITCH IN THE NEWS

by Michael Gleason

A number of years ago, I decided that it was time to clear up some of the public's misconceptions about Witchcraft. The logical thing to do, it seemed to me, was to arrange an interview with the local newspaper and explain things calmly and rationally. Given the way things normally worked in the town I lived in (Beverly, Massachusetts), I figured the interview would run in the Religion section on a Friday and that it might be seen by a limited number of people, but that it would be a good start.

I had what I considered to be a reasonably good interview with a reporter who seemed to grasp the concepts of what I was trying to get across. At the end of the interview I was asked if I would permit a photographer to come by that evening to get a few shots, one of which might be used in the article. I didn't see a problem with that, and agreed.

The photographer arrived and took photos of my wife and children (a son and daughter, both under the age of ten), in ritual robes, with altar and tools. After the photographer left, I relaxed and thought that it had all gone pretty well.

Imagine my surprise upon getting the paper a couple of days later to see our photo on the front page, with a multicolumn story continued to the back page. It seems it had been a slow news day, and it was approaching Halloween, so the editor ran the story under the headline "Ordinary People, Unusual Beliefs."

Still, I felt that things could have been much worse. The overall tone of the article was positive. It mentioned my involvement with the Parent-Teacher Organization at my children's school, the fact that both my wife and I were employed, and that we did our best to fit into the overall population of our community.

Well, of course, no good deed goes unpunished. Within a matter of days, my daughter began to be harassed by some of her classmates (to be fair, there weren't many, and the school staff did their best to defuse the situation), and letters to the editor appeared stating that we were obviously endangering the welfare of our children since we had dangerous weapons (a scourge, athame, and bolline) on the altar.

I was stopped by the school principal the next time I was in school, where I volunteered as a library assistant and read to a class of special needs children. He asked me to step into his office. He said, "I've been principal for over ten years and I don't ever remember getting calls from more than a couple of parents on any given situation in the school. Since that article ran, I've had a half a dozen calls demanding that you be removed from your position with the PTO since you are, in their opinion, a danger to the children. I told them that your religious beliefs have nothing to do with your function on the PTO. I also told them that if they wanted you removed, they would have to do it by a vote at a PTO meeting. I just felt you deserved a heads up." I thanked him and continued to the library for my shift.

A short while later, on her way home from school, my daughter, Sheri, was grabbed by a girl two years older than her and thrown to the ground in the street. She told Sheri that she better not put a curse on her. Naturally, we immediately contacted the school and arranged a meeting. The principal arranged for us to meet with the bully and her teacher. After we all settled in, he announced that since the assault didn't happen on school property he wouldn't be officially involved and left us to work it out.

The bully's teacher asked her why she had acted that way, and we were told that someone had told her that Sheri was going to put a curse on her, so she attacked Sheri. The teacher thought about it for a moment and then asked her, "If you thought Sheri was going to curse you, for no reason, wasn't it pretty foolish to do something that would make her even more likely to do it?" The girl didn't have an answer.

Then the teacher surprised us by asking the girl, "What do you know about Sheri's religion?" The girl started to respond, "Well, everybody knows . . . " but the teacher stopped her. "I didn't ask what 'everybody knows.' I asked what *you* knew." The girl admitted that she didn't know anything about Wicca, and again the teacher surprised us. He looked at her and announced, "I think you need to educate yourself. Therefore, first I expect you to apologize to Sheri, then I am giving you detention for a week, and I expect you to do a paper on what Witches believe."

The ultimate irony of that is that years later my daughter ran into the same girl while in Salem. The girl walked up to her and asked if Sheri remembered her. My daughter admitted that she didn't. The girl identified herself and pulled a small pentacle into view from around her neck. She had finished studying with a local group, and had become an initiate herself.

And, when a meeting was called by some of the PTO members on the subject of removing me from office, a friend of ours (who wasn't really comfortable with our religion) came up to me afterward and said, "I never realized how prejudiced some people can be. I heard people say 'You mean that Witch still wants to be part of the PTO?' and it occurred to me that they wouldn't have said 'You mean that Methodist (or Jehovah's Witness, or Jew, or . . .) still wants to be part of the PTO?' Your religion shouldn't have anything to do with it." She still wasn't really comfortable with our beliefs, but so long as we confined ourselves to nonreligious topics on both sides of the conversations, we got along fine from then on.

Although being a Witch has caused conflicts and problems with my family and the community that we live in, as the years go by, I have noticed that Witchcraft is actually beginning to become more mainstream. I am thrilled that my family was able to be a part of that and I am proud that we are Goddess worshippers.

KNOWING THE GOD AND
GODDESS THROUGH DAN

by Walter R. Hardin, Jr.

I was a Samhain baby, born October 31, 1966, in Louisville, Kentucky, at St. Anthony's Hospital. Suffice it to say that I grew up in the land of hardcore Christianity. I lived just east of Louisville with my parents, until their divorce when I was about four years old. It was just me, my mother, and three sisters living at home until my mother remarried, welcoming my stepfather and several stepsiblings into our home. My life consisted of going to church, sometimes six times in a week, and travelling to the family farm in Caneyville, Kentucky, to be weekend farmers.

The family farm was a seventy-three-acre lot with twenty-four acres of flat land for planting tobacco and corn. We harvested hay, as well, for the horses. As a young child, I remember going there on the weekends, and feeling very close to Mother Earth. I was starting to question what I was learning in church, but I could always come back to the farm and reconnect to the land and the horses. There was one horse in particular, Dan, my dad's chestnut quarter horse. Dan was not the tamest of horses, but he and I had a bond, and hit it off from the beginning. I would walk him whenever I could and I even learned to ride him. Dan and I developed our own little game. I called it the elephant game. Dan would lower his head so that I could lock my hands between his ears and then he would raise his head and lift me right off the ground. He would swing his head from left to right and my body would sway, just like an elephant's trunk. I was the only person he played that game with. Dan was one of the only constants in my life. I know that he was sent by the gods to be my companion because I never felt that I could talk to my parents. Whenever I tried, it was cause for physical and verbal abuse, so why bother?

Before my parents divorced, I was basically neglected by my biological mother. When my father remarried, and as I got older, it seemed that anything would set them off to physically abuse me. Missing my curfew because I didn't have a watch would result in getting punched and whipped (sometimes a rawhide whip and sometimes just a belt). One time I made the mistake of changing my prom date last minute, and the parents of the girl I dumped made a phone call to my folks and I ended up going to the prom with a broken nose, black eye, and bruises and cuts all over my body. Because of Dan, I was able to get through all of it, though. I spent several hours each day talking to Dan and telling him all of my problems. He had an incredible way of giving me a hug just when he knew that I needed one. He would lay his head over my left shoulder and I would throw my arms around his neck. I would feel the God and Goddess reaching out to me through this amazing horse and it made me feel so much better. I knew he was always there for me and the God and Goddess wanted to assure me of that. Dan guided me every day that I was on that farm and I thank the Earth Mother for the time I spent there with him. It's where I learned to meditate and to become one with the Earth.

Dan was like a brother and we had one thing in common; we were both abused by my father. Dan was stubborn, and my father had a whip in the barn with metal ends. Every time Dan went back to the barn against my father's wishes, he would whip poor Dan between the ears until he was bleeding. My heart bled as well, and as I was only three years old when I first saw it, the images made a dramatic impact on me and my life. I think Dan and I both learned to help each other feel better when we were together, and there was always a mutual respect and sympathy between us. We grew up enduring the abuse together, and bonded in like mind and camaraderie.

Several years later, after serving time in the Army and while still serving in the Army reserve, I happened upon a huge new bookstore in Louisville. I remember walking in the door and being mystically led right to the New Age section, where I immediately made eye contact with Scott Cunningham's *Wicca: A Guide for the Solitary Practitioner*. I purchased the book and read it in record time. The strange thing for me was that it felt so familiar, like I already knew it. I was already living it. However, I still kept my secret. If I told anyone, I knew they would be very hateful and mean to me. I would have no more friends. As far as I knew, I was alone and with no one to talk to about my feelings and beliefs.

Shortly after that, I bought my very first computer. It took me a few months, but I finally figured out the Internet. I found an AOL chat room called The Metaphysics Room. Wow! I had found my cyber home. Finally, I was not alone! I met a girlfriend through the Internet, and yes, she was a Witch. I moved to Detroit to be with her. She introduced me to Pagan and Goth music. She taught me about Wicca and my spiritual path. We went to Salem, Massachusetts, together. On this trip I met Laurie Cabot, found the pentacle necklace that called out to me, and made the choice to come out of the broom closet as a birthday gift to myself that Samhain. Soon after, I went to a seminar on Wicca and met Gavin and Yvonne Frost. I also attended a meditation seminar and learned that Dan was my spirit guide. He had made his peaceful passing in September of 1998. I deeply miss him, but now I know that Dan will always be with me.

I did go back home to tell all of my family that I'm a Witch. This went better than expected. Mama (my dad's mother) just frowned and said that she will continue to pray that I am saved and will go to Heaven when I die. My biological mother and stepfather shook their heads in disbelief, and when I told my dad and stepmother on the farm, he laughed, and she said the lowest, softest, gentlest voice I had ever heard from her mouth, "It's okay, Ray. It's just a phase that you will grow out of." Well, I was in my early thirties at the time and I still haven't grown out of this phase yet.

I never was very accepted by my family anyway. So I don't miss them much and they pretty much don't think about me. But that's okay. I have my own family now. We are all Witches and are very active with our friends in the Pagan community. And one thing I know for sure is that I will always have the God and Goddess and Dan!

WORLDWIDE WITCHES

by Amy Midnight

I grew up in a Muslim family in Singapore. Islam has always taught that other religions worship the Devil and I was taught that only Muslims worship a true God. Wicca is not widely known where I lived. There are no Wiccan stores and one certainly can't find books about Wicca there, but ever since I was young I have always been fascinated with the supernatural and magic. Although I was a Muslim then, I felt a certain connection with Witchcraft. I wasn't sure why, but the idea of sitting in the center of a ring of candles excited me. Fire has always fascinated me, and I became so fond of candles. As time passed, I couldn't help but feel uneasy though. I just couldn't shake the thought that I was entering the dark unknown. There was always that constant nag of a second voice reminding me of my betrayal of my religion. I still pursued Witchcraft, seeking for something to feel connected to, a belonging of sorts. It sucked me in and I liked being special and I loved the feeling of being perpetually energized.

As I got older I was able to find books about Witchcraft. I learned a lot and started dabbling with it. I started with simple meditations, protection spells, and luck spells. I had even done a spell to make someone kiss me and another one to make them forget that they ever saw me. I know that I was messing with their free will, but I didn't real- ize it then. Most of the spells were successful, but like any new Witch discovers, some just didn't work.

Then my parents found out about my dabbling! They were furi- ous. I told them that I was only doing research to write a story. It was half true. After that episode, they were under the impression that I had stopped the nonsense and returned to being a Muslim, but there were too many rules that I didn't agree with. It didn't work for me! My parents were constantly nagging at me. They would forever talk about their religion and tell me "you can't do this because you're a Muslim" or "you can't do that because you're a Muslim." I felt myself pulling far away from Islam and closer to Witchcraft.

As I was researching, I discovered that Wicca was actually a Witch- craft religion. I picked up a good book by Jamie Wood entitled *The Teen Spell Book: Magic for Young Witches*. The book taught about basic spells and what you should know when taking steps to perform them. From there I began to learn the different traditions and found myself pulled toward the Celtic tradition.

But then I found myself sinking, as I was stuck in between two religions. It was a constant battle from within and that was when the Goddess came to help me. She opened up my eyes and my heart just enough so that I could listen to my personal truths! I had been only pretending to be a Muslim and all this time I was never happy with who I was. The Goddess helped me realize that I had to choose my own path, not someone else's. For the first time in my life, I had to be true to myself! I became a Wiccan and travelled on the path only bringing with me fear and doubt. I just wasn't able to shake it. I was alone and worried. In this most trying time, I sought the Goddess's help again, and she assured me that I would receive guidance soon. She was so right!

Shortly after receiving that message from the Goddess, I met a friend online. Cassie and I instantly became best sisters. It was like we had known each other forever and we still managed to get closer with each passing day. Then we were blessed to find Thomas, another online friend. Together, the three of us and the rest of Thomas' friends started an online coven. This coven is my gift; my guidance that the Goddess promised me! I can't believe that I once walked this path alone! We practice within the Celtic Tradition and spread perfect love and perfect trust to all we come in contact with. Our coven has grown and together we share our knowledge and experiences. Together we were able to fight out of the darkness and emerge into the light. I will forever cherish the loving support I receive from my coven mates. They aren't just friends, they are my family! They've shown me love, they've helped me accept myself, and they've always encouraged me to be myself. Every day I wake up looking forward to talking to them, smiling and laughing with them, praying with them, and feeling their energy and comfort. They are my inspiration and my miracle!

Today my doubts about Wicca have completely dissolved and my faith has strengthened. Though I know that I will lose my biological family by being a Wiccan, I am glad that I have been given Wicca as a gift from the Goddess. Through Wicca, I have been taught to see the world and life in a new way and accept life more positively than ever before. Every single bad thing or any suffering that I may encounter encourages me to look forward to the reason behind it. I have been put through so many tests. I have never failed though, because I have never wavered from my faith in the Goddess. Wicca is a religion that makes us happy about ourselves and does not condemn us for sins. I trust in the Goddess and I pray for others that they will trust in her too.

PROTECTED

by Delia E. Halnen-On

When I was about twelve, my mother began to take me to a Baptist church. I will admit that I felt the presence of something there, but I wasn't sure if it was God or not. Intuitively, though, I knew that there was more to this whole religion thing than what was being preached to me on those Sunday mornings. But I was at a loss for words and unable to describe what I was feeling. I read the Bible and wondered: How could any of this be true? Where was the Goddess? If there truly was a God, then there had to be a Goddess.

In my limited view of the world, I knew that there were differences. Even something as simple as male and female was evident to me. I had been told many times by different people that we were made in God's own image. To my mind that explained the male aspect of the human race, but what about the female? Whose image were we created from? We don't look like men, so therefore we must be made from someone else's image. I felt that as a girl, I must be made from the Goddess's image. I believed that to have a God, you must have a Goddess, because in order to have a baby you needed a mother and a father.

In my discovery of mythology later in life, I found the Goddess I had been searching for. The goddesses that were described in mythology gave me an incredible amount of hope that there were actually people out there, just like me, who once believed in Her. That was enough for me to know, and I never really felt the need to learn more.

At least not until my freshman year of high school, when I was involved in a severe car accident, which left me with a fractured pelvis and serious nerve damage. While walking home from school one cold and rainy March day, I was hit from behind by a car driven by another student in the schoolyard. I was sent about ten feet into the air and came crashing down head first on the wet pavement. When I sat up and looked around, I saw that the vehicle that had hit me stopped at the bottom of the hill. Four, maybe five people, had gotten out of the car and were now staring at me with looks of shock and horror on their faces.

It was really strange though, in those few seconds before my impact with the ground. I felt protected, like someone was actually holding me. Once I hit the ground, I went into shock. I became confused and everything seemed so surreal, like a bad dream. In the ambulance on the way to the hospital, time seemed to stand still as the medical technicians kept drilling me with all kinds of questions. I was having trouble answering them because I couldn't think clearly. I was confused. But, one thing was very clear as it ran through my mind over and over again: *Thank you, Goddess.* It didn't even occur to me to thank God! I knew it was the Divine Mother who was protecting me. I was still alive due to her love and compassion. When they wheeled my stretcher into the emergency room they placed me under a clock. As I watched the time slowly ticking by, confined within the restraints of the collar brace and backboard, there was no doubt in my mind that I was safe and that the doctors were going to treat my wounds. I felt the Goddess's loving arms around me, keeping me warm and secure.

After my broken bones had healed, I began the constant struggle of three or four days a week of physical therapy. During that time, I felt that same protection surrounding me, pushing me to keep going. Whenever I felt myself wanting to give up, a little voice would whisper, "No, you can't! Keep going! You can do it!" After many months of rehabilitation, my bones healed, and I regained the ability to walk without a limp.

The day of that accident and the months of rehabilitation that followed finally convinced me that there truly is a Goddess. Until she revealed herself to me in my time of need, I had doubts that she really existed. I can't even begin to put into words what it was like to be in the close presence of such a powerful force.

Many years later, I discovered Wicca through a classmate in college who practiced it. I found that my own personal beliefs, which had formed over the years, were consistent with those of the Wiccan faith. How blessed I was to have found this out. I no longer had to keep my beliefs bottled up inside for fear that no one else would understand them. From that point on I stopped wondering and instead I simply asked the Goddess, "Is this the faith for me?" I waited, listened, and in a very quiet whisper that was all too familiar to me, I heard a very clear and definitive, "Yes."

EVOLUTION AND OUTREACH

by Gina Ellis

Looking back, I see several stages in the evolution of the attitude toward Wicca on the part of the media and society, and by people toward me as a Wiccan. The first stage was incredulity and suspicion, perhaps even a little fear. When I started thirty years ago, the reaction was, "Wicca—what's that? *Witchcraft?* Ooooh."

I probably told only my then-husband, who was duly incredulous and suspicious—"this must be some damned feminist plot." And, in fact, I came to Wicca through a friend I'd met at the feminist Consciousness Raising group I belonged to at the time.

Just previously, I had happened into a public lecture by Naomi Goldenberg at Carleton University on the then-new Goddess movement. It was exciting (and oddly familiar; I realized later that I'd read Gardner's *Witchcraft Today* when it first came out) and so when I saw a notice in a women's paper about a coven forming, I phoned . . . and found myself talking to someone from my Consciousness Raising group. We started circling together, and I had the archetypical "coming home" experience. I've stayed "home" ever since, even if sometimes distressed by my relatives.

We were somewhat fearful ourselves, my Priestess and I, as to what kind of men might want to join a coven, so we only looked for other women. This was despite my Priestess being a variety of what these days is called British Traditional (that is, descended from Gerald Gardner, as distinguished from the better-known eclectic Wicca), a practice that requires both men and women.

Nevertheless, we soon achieved proper gender balance, although our female recruits didn't last. On a trip to Montreal, my High Priestess visited an occult bookstore and hit it off with the proprietor, who was looking for something simpler and more natural than his ceremonial practice. And he knew some other interested people. Thus was born the Silver Wheel coven, which is still going strong today, though I am the only remaining original member.

We were properly secretive, and not just with respect to non-Wiccans. I remember attending the first Earth Spirit gathering in Massachusetts, where people were edgy. It was like a convention of porcupines, happy to be together but very cautious when it came to comparing notes.

Back home, it came to my attention that there were other Wiccans in the Ottawa area, and I started attending a moot. I also discovered WicCanFest, which was located quite a few hours away. It was suggested, since I lived on an acreage, that we have a small local fest at my place, and thus, with a first attendance of about 45, Mini-Fest was born. After a few years, when 300 people were turning up to camp on my couple of acres of stone, bush and swamp, I found another site for them and bid the fest merry part. It continued to grow and has become the very successful Kaleidoscope.

The next stage in public attitude toward Wicca was ridicule. Fortunately we Wiccans don't take ourselves too seriously, or at least don't stand on our dignity. I suppose any non-Pagan who knew I was Wiccan thought it was funny. But there didn't seem any need to talk about my religion. And I was never one for the jewelry and flowing skirts: I could pass as normal.

I didn't encounter hostility, although there are no secrets out here in the country. I did run into a man one day strolling through my garden, telling his small son that this was the witch's house. But my neighbor was fine about Mini-Fest using his pasture for our main ritual, and the municipal office was fine with occasionally renting their meeting room to us for rainy Sabbats. The local arts and recreation group even asked if we'd like Mini-Fest listed in its calendar of events.

The next stage was treating Wicca as a recognized religion, though with some stifled snickering or indignation. That was the attitude when I moved into doing prison work. I found myself mentioned, and not in a good way, on the front page of the *National Post* and featured in a couple of snarky columns in some of the *Sun* chain of papers. The Corrections Canada people who ran the penitentiaries, however, treated us like any other religious group, albeit with the occasional joke about witches or spells. The law on religious accommodation for people in custody brought both them and us into an unexpected relationship.

But being treated like other groups were brought up a problem. Corrections Canada does not deal with individual religious people, but, understandably, with organizations that are accountable for their prison visitors. That works fine with mainstream religions that are already set up to work that way. So when my colleague and I took over the Kingston-area prisons, we were required to get organizational backing.

Thus began my public, respectable, and "normal" period, and a not entirely successful experiment in trying to stuff anarchic Paganism into mainstream-like structures.

My prison colleague and I took our need for a sponsoring organization to a handful of active Ottawa Wiccans. We were all of different paths, so could not form a church—and didn't want to. We settled on putting together a common-interest body, the Pagan Federation/*Federation païenne Canada* (PFPC). It was inspired by the Pagan Federation in the United Kingdom. and for a while was loosely affiliated with them.

I persisted with PFPC for many years in the face of indifference on the part of most Pagans, and eventually, because my main purpose was to meet the prison requirements, I left it for a scaled-down focused spinoff, the still-current Pagan Pastoral Outreach. Ironically, over the years hospitals and prisons and other bodies seem to have pretty much resigned themselves to dealing with Pagans on our own individual terms instead of with a formal organization. However, I still see some dangers in having people with no accountability to a larger community representing us in an official capacity in the public arena.

Through the prisons, I got involved with a regional branch of the Ontario Multifaith Council, a body that oversees religious accommodation in provincial institutions. There, Wicca was accepted as just another religion by all the others, though the Scientologist seemed to think she and I needed to stick together.

Prison visitation has grown over the years. I'm on an Internet group with nearly one hundred members, mostly in the United States, ministering to as many of the thousands of Pagan inmates as possible. Most Pagan inmates came to their religion inside their institution, in what looks like the same proportion to the general population on the outside. Pagans tended to disapprove of community involvement with prisons to begin with, but the idea has gained some support over the years. For my part, it introduced me to people I'd never normally have met; not just convicted criminals (who turned out to be not all that different from anybody else), but also chaplains of various denominations who changed some of my negative ideas about Christians. There was a Mennonite minister who talked about the Pagan Christ, and a Catholic chaplain who asked our inmate group to remember one of his dead at Samhain. Some chaplains have sat in on rituals or even taken part. In Quebec, one translated for me when the guard at the front desk wanted a Tarot reading. Another actually took up Tarot, seeing how useful it was in getting inmates to talk . . . and to listen.

My happiest memory of my prison outreach was helping the inmates in grim, grey Kingston Penitentiary to get outdoors, where eventually they were able to re-sod an area and plant a border of flowers. In the chapel area of a couple of other Kingston prisons, the Pagan groups were also allowed small flower gardens.

Time moves on. The next attitude toward Wicca seemed to be acceptance as something harmless. There are still some eruptions of fear from the fundamentalist outskirts, some amusement or morbid interest in the media, but essentially we're just part of the variegated cultural landscape, and officially counted in the census.

This normalization was reflected in my next activity, the Canadian National Pagan Conference. I and my colleague in this dealt with booking universities as low-cost venues, with no weirdness. Well, why not? At the first conference, at the University of Alberta in 2004, we were booked right after a rope-skipping convention!

The conference included an academic stream for papers presented by the numerous Pagans studying and teaching in universities, where this new religious movement is a topic of interest. The first conference, in Edmonton, and the third, in Winnipeg, featured Canadian non-Pagan authors whose books were about Pagans (Kevin Marron, author of *Witches, Pagans and Magic in the New Age*) or had a theme of interest (Tim Ward, author of *Savage Breast*, about men and the Goddess). The 2006 conference in Halifax featured Canadian Pagan authors Shelley Rabinovitch and Brendan Myers.

I put in a three-year term on the conference, working on protocols, coming up with the guest speakers, overseeing the website, working out the idea of participatory panels (as opposed to a series of single speakers), and keeping a national and serious focus (no whacked-out workshops). The conference still continues. The fourth conference took place in Ottawa in 2008, and the 2009 conference in Vancouver. The 2010 conference is scheduled to take place in Guelph.

The current stage of acceptance of Wicca is the acknowledgment by society of what we have in common. This isn't a unanimous position; there are holdouts back at all the earlier stages, and even some people who haven't even heard of us. But in the vanguard are people—of other religions and no religion—who have parallel interest in the ideas of the Feminine Divine, of Gaia, the Earth as a living entity, of environmentalism and the need to connect with Nature, of the need to have celebrations and rituals to mark the stations of life and the stations of the year, of spiritual autonomy, of coming together without dogma and hierarchy . . .

I guess in a way that's also the stage I'm at: a kind of post-Wicca, no longer struggling with structures and people. I continue with the venerable Silver Wheel that keeps rollin' on. I circle with local people, most of whom do not label themselves as Wiccan but feel a need to celebrate the changes of the seasons and meditate under the moon. My daughter and I host a small gathering (Micro-Fest), which offers no workshops, just an opportunity to relax at season's end . . . and an excuse for us to hire a band to play in our backyard!

Perhaps there will be further stages: the institutionalization of Wicca, the creation of formal seminaries, the affectation of calling ourselves Reverend, and the mainstreaming of Wicca as a result of our ever-increasing numbers. All of this would leave me behind, content with the experiences I have had with other Wiccans and as a Wiccan *vis-à-vis* the outer world. Some of it was fun, some of it was heartbreaking, but it's all grist for the mill of the gods.

At Peace with Wicca

by Steven Prince

Religion, in my opinion, seems like the ability to dance. Some people have it, and can move like gods. Some people couldn't (or wouldn't) dance if you hooked them to a car battery and shocked them. Most people look at those who can dance, try to copy them, and then kid themselves that they're as good at it as the next person. I've always thought that last category of people were the worst. It takes a lot of courage to have both faith and a lack of faith, but it's too easy to follow everyone else without thinking for yourself.

I can't remember at what age I started questioning my faith (or intermittent lack thereof). I was raised Roman Catholic—God is great (but full of angry wrath), Heaven, Hell, the whole nine yards (or Ten Commandments). I think a turning point was when my parents got divorced. I was only ten, but I couldn't understand how a so-called loving God could let this happen. After thinking about it, I really started to understand why some people could say that Catholics mourn their faith. My faith had always felt like a burden to me, because every Sunday at 11:00 A.M. (and during every day at Catholic school until I was eighteen), I was reminded that pretty much everything I did, said, and thought at some point or another was a sin.

Growing up in a small country town in Australia wasn't exactly conducive to religious experimentation. Luckily, I'm the youngest of four children, and my mother was very supportive of us and the choices we made. The key for me should have been that every time I went to church, I struggled to stay awake. It's not that I didn't appreciate what Jesus apparently did for me, it's just that the apparent flame of faith didn't ever do anything more than flicker before going out.

For a long time, I avoided religion as a whole. After many years, I couldn't find a path that I could identify with. While I could certainly understand and support the basic underlying tenants—do unto others, killing is bad, and so on—I couldn't get comfortable with the idea of being told how and when to worship. In my mind, I felt that anyone who was worth me praying to should understand that I needed the freedom to express how I related to them.

I'd heard about Wicca for the first time when I was at college. I must admit that the first exposure I had to it seemed kind of weird—it seemed to consist of girls (and guys for that matter) wearing eyeliner, using Ouija boards, and dressing in dark clothes while trying to seem dark and mysterious. Not exactly the best way to make a good first impression!

I only started to really understand it when I met my fiancée. She was Wiccan, and she encouraged me to go to a church meeting, meet her minister, and see if maybe it was for me. I still remember my first service—a metaphysical one with meditation, songs, and a sermon. It really wasn't at all what I expected after my experience in college. The service was held in a finished basement of a very nice home in a very affluent town. This sanctuary had painted murals on each wall depicting the elements. The north wall displayed beautiful mountains and evergreen trees, which represented the earth. The south wall had an incredible more than life-like dragon that you could just imagine blowing the most fierce and deadly fire from the depth of his insides. The east wall just had subtle paintbrush strokes to give the very real feeling of wind blowing. And the west wall displayed a very calming and serene lake surrounded by trees and rocks. The murals were so life-like that I truly felt like I was outside and free. I wish I could put into words how all of this made me feel, but I can't.

I remember closing my eyes and finally feeling peace. The screaming, frantic pace of the world slowed, and I was able to actually hear my own thoughts for the first time in a long time. The smiles I saw on faces were genuine, and the sermon came from a place of love and compassion, not out of a need to remind people that they were born a sinner, lived in sin and would most likely die in sin unless they were very lucky. I know that I'm coming off as a jaded cynic. Well, I am. I find it very hard to believe for the sake of belief—I need to be able to identify with what I'm supposed to believe in, and until I experienced Wicca, I wasn't able to find that. Putting all my faith in one theological basket requires a mind more trusting than mine. That being said, I can without doubt accept the circle of life, and that there is a connection and interplay between humanity and our Earth.

While I'm still waiting for the bolt of religious inspiration to hit me, I still think of Wicca as my most logical future path. Luckily, my family knows of my fiancée's religious beliefs, and they know I'm also interested in where my spiritual path may lead. They're certainly as loving and as accepting as I could ask for, although it's taken them a little convincing to believe that their frog's legs and newt's eyes are safe around us, and that we don't get naked and howl at the moon. Well, at least not in the name of religion, anyway.

I can honestly say that after experiencing Wicca in the way that I did with my fiancée, for the first time in quite a while, I have faith.

PLAYING WITH THE WIND

by Bob Chipman

I was nine years old and I had a brand new kite and no wind. I didn't know what I was doing, but I knew that the wind liked to play with the autumn leaves, so I picked up a few fallen leaves and tossed them in the air and said, "Come play with me." The winds came, and I flew my kite.

Even as a kid, I knew magic was real. I could feel it when I would walk through the woods; I could feel it when I would walk along the beach. I have always been close to nature and always felt connected to the energy around me. It was in nature that I felt Magic, and it was in nature that I felt Deity.

My parents were what you would call nonpracticing Christians. They were good people, just not church-going people. So they were surprised when at the age of fifteen, I started going to a local Bible church. Now this wasn't just your basic church, this was a Christian-fundamentalist, fire-and-brimstone, Bible-believing, salvation-preaching, hallelujah-Jesus church, and I could feel the same type of energy within that church as I did in nature. Knowing that my parents were

Christian, I thought this was an acceptable way to celebrate my spirituality while still feeling connected to the magic around me.

It was during my teen years that I started feeling that I should be doing more. I became more involved with the various programs the church had to offer, helping in Sunday School and also, the Bus ministry. I attended a Christian college and started working in various Christian ministries. And yet, I was still missing something, I felt incomplete. I still had a lot of questions.

I kept studying things like Native American beliefs, Buddhism, Eastern Philosophy, Taoism, and Wicca. Each one of them sparked an interest within me. Each had pieces to the puzzle I was trying to put together.

I finally reached a point where I felt I had to make a decision. There were a lot of things that just didn't make sense to me, and the more I studied, the more I felt what I was teaching others in church wasn't what I personally believed. I had been taught, and so was teaching, that Magic was wrong and that all other religions were wrong; that Christianity was the only true path to God. I would constantly ask, "Why?" The answers I was given never really answered my questions, they just created more questions. I was basically taught to just accept the way it was and blindly. But, I knew that I couldn't just do that.

During that time, I had decided to take some time off from teaching in the church and to spend more time walking through the woods and along the beach. I meditated, and studied, and prayed, and I walked and walked. I could feel the wind against me and had this gnawing feeling that I should be remembering something. And as I found myself walking off one path and onto another, I said it for the first time, "I am a Pagan and I am a Witch." I felt like a weight had been lifted from my back and for the first time in a long time, I felt right. It was an epiphany. The puzzle pieces came together in my life, and for the first time, I knew what I believed, and it wasn't what I had thought I believed. And then I wondered, "What do I do now?"

A little over two years is how long it took for me to make the decision to become an open Pagan. I continued to study, to pray, and to walk. I knew where I was supposed to be and what I was supposed to do, but figuring out how to tell people was the hard part.

I knew the surprise my parents felt when I told them, at the age of fifteen, that I was going to church. I knew that reaction was nothing compared to the surprise they would have when I told them, at the age of thirty-seven, that I was a Pagan Witch, but when the time came I just told them. I consider myself a very fortunate man to have the family that I have. They asked a lot of questions and I was ready with the answers. In the end, the way they think of me hasn't changed a bit.

I don't believe in coincidence and happenstance. I was ordained as a Pagan minister in 2005 and my time in the Christian ministry gave me a lot of skills that translated well into my Pagan ministry. I find that the Lord and Lady bring me a lot of interfaith work and I feel that I am right where I am supposed to be. It has been over eight years since I found my path and I still remember the question that I asked then, and I also remember the answer that the wind gave me: "Come play with me." I have played with the wind ever since.

CONNECTED

by Blade

I guess I should start by saying I was not one of those people who always felt something was missing. I wasn't good with animals, and I definitely wasn't in tune with nature from the beginning. If anything, I was just the opposite. The first Earth Day I can recall was spent scrapping an acre to make way for the new house. My second not-so-in-touch-with-nature story involves the day my brother and I really did find the end of a rainbow. It landed right at the foot of a small maple sapling whose leaves had all turned a gold color. They were promptly stripped and used as currency in whatever game we were playing that afternoon. Maybe it's guilty memories like this that moved me toward a more nature-based faith system.

I first became aware of the notion of witchcraft as something people seriously followed while I was in high school. It wasn't actually the fluff films of that period that caught my attention, but some piece I happened to catch on *Unsolved Mysteries*. I poked around in the family encyclopedia set after seeing that segment but couldn't find anything that matched up and promptly forgot about the whole thing for a year or so until stumbling upon Laurie Cabot's *Power of the Witch* at the public library. I read through it and somehow came to the conclusion that my math teacher was a witch. I stuck around after class one day and asked her point blank if she could teach me what she knew about all sorts of topics that I can now hardly recall, although I do know magic was in that rapid-fire list. This is where I consider my journey down a Neo-Pagan path to have begun.

I didn't learn anything about magic as I viewed it at the time from that great lady. Nor did she have anything to offer pertaining to the Craft. She had promised her late father never to study witchcraft, and never broke her word. But she knew that what I was looking for was not the same craft her father had warned her against. What she did teach me was probably far more important then I could possibly understand at the time. She always seemed to know exactly which book would serve me best at the time. *The Way of the Peaceful Warrior* by Dan Millman was the first thing she had me read, followed by its sequel. *The Tao of Pooh* was read somewhere in that year, too, along with so many others I've long forgotten the titles of. While most of the material she provided me was of a philosophical nature, there were some oddballs in the lot. *Shibumi* is one of the latter works that immediately comes to mind. Apart from giving me books that made me re-examine my perecption of the world around me, she also started what became a semi-private Tai-Chi and meditation club. I call it semi-private because it was only me and one of the librarians who always went. This teacher gave me more than I could ever thank her for: she encouraged me to look into Eastern and alternative philosophy to better understand the world around me.

After graduating from high school, I began pursuing my interest in witchcraft once again. This time armed with a computer and Internet access, I was able to track down some message boards as well as the local metaphysical supply shop. I signed up for some workshops and read everything I could get my hands on. It was around this time that I began associating myself with the term *technopagan*. Initially it was because I was one of the few people I knew who insisted on digital records of everything, but it rapidly expanded into exploring the notion of magic as it related to a world that people used to only understand in abstract metaphysical terms. I kept reading about how everyone was connected as a spiritual abstract, when in reality that world existed right in front of me. Paganism, in a broad stroke, is about embracing nature around you. Technopaganism to me just seems like a natural extension from that to embracing the technology around me. This approach is actually the source of most of the resistance to my beliefs. Pagans in general tend to be much more focused on the natural world. The notion of incorporating modern convenience into my practices is often smirked at, if not outright sneered at. I've always found it sadly ironic that a group of people that often complains about being marginalized and discriminated against is just as guilty of said offenses.

The whole notion of coming out of the broom closet seemed like a monumental step when I first read about it. I guess what pushed me was that raw human need to share things that make a person happy, coupled with some adolescent need to establish oneself as one's own person. My mom was the first person I told and was actually the only one I was nervous about. She took a moment to process what I had just told her, then said that I was a stable individual who didn't do crazy things, so I must have a solid and understandable explanation for her. I loaned her one of the simpler books I had acquired and she gave it back after a few chapters with some kind of "whatever makes you happy, dear" comment. I went on to tell most of my family in some fashion over the course of a few months after that. Oftentimes it was off the cuff when the right situation presented itself, and was pretty much met with some sort of comment about that making sense about me. The ones I didn't actively tell found out in some way at my handfasting. From what I've heard, the family that knew about my spiritual path warned those who didn't that it wasn't going to be a normal wedding in advance of the event. My grandparents were the only ones I'd have been concerned about, but they enjoyed the different ceremony which was held outdoors. My sister's simple Hindu wedding the previous summer might have helped smooth the way for the general acceptance of the alternative wedding ceremony, but I guess I'll never truly know. As far as friends and coworkers go, my religion is not something I mention unless it's the topic at hand and I'm directly asked. It isn't something I hide, nor is it something I feel the need to advertise to the world. I've always been something of an introvert, which partially explains why I mostly keep to myself and don't share my views with everyone. I do co-lead a private group with my wife, however, who is a very active community leader in her own right. I mostly function in a supportive role.

In the end, there's only one major challenge I've had to face: The resistance to my views from within the Pagan community itself, and not the general public. If anything, the fact that my approach to Paganism encompasses the modern world helps when I do have to explain it to someone who doesn't understand what it's all about.

THE BRIGHTEST LIGHT IN THE DARKEST TIME

by Elena M. Kelley (in memory of Diane T. Kelley-Marchesini)

The last lucid conversation I had with my mother is burned in my brain.

I received a frantic phone call during dinner. My mother had been evicted from her apartment and needed a place to stay for a while. After discussing the situation with my roommate and working out some ground rules, I called her back and told her that she could move in with us the next day. Wednesday morning, my mother and I gathered her belongings and made our way to my apartment. All of a sudden she tripped and fell. She had been falling a lot over the previous few weeks, and she had been brushing it off like nothing was wrong. When we got to the bus stop, she suddenly got cold. It was a nice August day, and she was wearing a hooded sweatshirt, but she was covered in goose bumps and shivering. Less than five minutes later, she claimed that she saw a wild dog in the sewer at the bus stop. This was when I knew something was seriously wrong and immediately called 911. Once I told my mother that the ambulance was on its way, she said, "They can come as long as they bring ice cream."

When the ambulance arrived, one of the EMTs asked my mother a series of questions and her answers were nothing more than gibberish. The one thing that was clear was the name of the hospital she wanted to be taken to. My roommate left work immediately and joined me in the emergency room. About an hour later, my mother's best friend, who I have always considered to be an aunt, arrived at the hospital. All that was left to do was wait. And wait. We all knew something was seriously wrong when we were pulled into a small room just off the emergency room and told that the doctor wanted to speak to us. We were told that my mother had gone into full cardiac arrest for more than five minutes. She was being transferred to ICU soon. When I heard this, I felt like I was going to be sick. The room was spinning; I broke out in a cold sweat, and I was shaking. It was all too much for me. The diagnosis made my heart ache. It started as a simple urinary tract infection that turned into septicemia, and I was told that she might not make it.

When we left the family room in the hospital, I was shocked to find friends and family waiting for us. Nearly everyone from the Wiccan church I attended had either shown up or called. They stayed as long as they could, and headed out for the night. My aunt, my roommate, and I settled in for a long night in the ICU waiting room.

Friday afternoon, my High Priestess, who is also a minister, arrived just to sit with us. The first thing that she did when she got to the hospital was to give me the biggest hug that I have ever had, and she assured me that no matter what happened, the God and Goddess would protect me and my family. Most of the day consisted of crying, laughing, and remembering the legacy my mother brought. That evening my mother's neurologist came to see me. He told us that my mother showed no signs of higher brain function and would not wake up. All I could do was cry. I vaguely remember the neurologist apologizing for our loss. I remember so many hands on me, not from my family, but from my aunt and my many friends from church who were there just because they cared. My fiancé arrived from Australia late that night, and I was so grateful to see him walk through the door. By Sunday afternoon, it was time to let Mom go. I remember a blur of people coming into her hospital room to say their final goodbyes before we took her off life support. My family had gathered, as had practically my entire church. I sat outside her hospital room with my aunt, my roommate, and my fiancé, knowing that family and my minister were at her bedside when everything was turned off. It was 2:20 in the afternoon. I thought it would be a quick process, but by 10:30 P.M., Mom was still holding on. My minister looked at all of our tired faces and listened to the most absurd things that would send us into fits of giggles, and concluded that we desperately needed sleep. So, we heeded her advice and headed home. We were home for barely five minutes when we got the call that my mother had died. I flew back to the hospital so I could say a final goodbye, but I just couldn't bring myself to walk into her room. In five short days, Mom had gone from being a vibrant, happy-go-lucky person who could slug her way through anything, to being gone.

Looking back at it now I realize that through this experience, I felt the God and Goddess, not through my blood family, but through my chosen family. And although I had been a brat just as recently as two weeks before that, I saw nothing but unconditional love in the eyes of those around me.

In a time of crisis, we banded together. During my vigil at the hospital, nearly every single parishioner came to sit with me; some bringing games and books to provide a distraction, while others brought food, because they suspected I wasn't eating much. They were all there when I needed them most, and that's what counts. I could see the God and Goddess in each person's eyes while they were there in my time of greatest need. While the last member of my immediate family may be gone, I know that the God and Goddess will always be there for me as they manifest themselves in the faces of those who are closest to me. I never could have gotten through the loss of my mother without them and I will always be thankful that they knew just how to reach me in my time of need. Through the greatest loss of my life, thanks to the unconditional love of the God and Goddess, I realize just how much I have to live for.

My First Tattoo

by Shoshana E. Berman

Pretty much all of my life, I realized that I thought of religion quite differently than the rest of my Jewish family. I knew that there just had to be something more than what we were taught. Although I treasure my Jewish heritage, I now consider myself to be a Wiccan Jew, or what some might label a Jewitch. I never knew the name for what I believed in until about five years ago. I was actually shopping on eBay and was fortunate enough to have met a wonderful woman who sent me in the direction that I now call my religion. I am a solitary practitioner, and consider myself to be very much a novice who is fortunate enough to have some wonderful friends who guide me. It's great to have friends who I can talk so openly and freely with.

Once I made the decision that this path was right for me, I dedicated myself to the ways and teachings of the Goddess by getting my very first tattoo. It's a small one located on the back of my shoulder: a triple Goddess, with a pentacle inside the full moon. Around the same time that my husband bought me this beautiful tattoo, we were all preparing for a baby shower. My son's wife was pregnant and expecting her first child. I was so excited for the upcoming birth of my grand-daughter, Emma! My son and his wife put a huge damper on things, though, by insisting that my shoulder be covered prior to any guests arriving to their house. I did bring a wrap with me and planned on covering it up once I finished preparations around the house. Little did I know that what they really meant to say was, "Cover your tattoo before you set foot on our property." What happened next was like something from a horror movie. My daughter-in-law started ranting and raving that I was a psycho and worshipped the Devil! She said that only sick people do what I am doing and then my son started in on me. He yelled, "How dare you set foot in our house with your shoulder uncovered and that tattoo in plain sight of all our guests!" Tattoos were the mark of the Devil, they kept screaming at me. They kicked me and my husband out of the house, and we cried the entire way home. I was in shock. We had spent so much time and money on a baby shower that all of our friends would be at, and now we weren't even allowed to attend. About an hour later my son called and begged us to come back, so long as I was properly dressed. "Properly dressed by whose standards?" I wondered. In an effort to keep the peace, I changed and my husband and I went back, but things were never the same after that. My daughter-in-law actually took the handmade quilt I made for the baby and tossed it to the side without ever even opening it. To this day, I can't move beyond that!

The bottom line in all of this is that once I came out of the broom closet I lost all rights to ever see my oldest son and his children. My grandchildren! My son's wife is a Christian Fundamentalist and is convinced that both my husband and I worship the Devil. My son thinks that all of the Yankee Candle jars I have around the house are for holding séances, and my daughter-in-law has convinced him that any pictures that I have of my granddaughter are being used in Witchcraft.

Today Emma is four years old and I have a new grandson named David. My son and daughter-in-law will not allow me to see them or have any contact with them. I am not allowed to meet my new grandson, and I cannot have any pictures of him either. To say that my heart is broken is a huge understatement.

There is just no way to reach people who are so close minded. They refuse to move on and just accept people as being different and love them for who and what they are. How is that being a good Christian?

I feel that I have lost all control and have virtually no hope left in me. We continually get nasty phone calls from my daughter-in-law about being witches. My husband doesn't even practice Wicca! I guess it is bad enough that he supports me in my beliefs. Even my Rabbi sees nothing wrong with me and my beliefs, and has given me his blessing.

We have been told that under no uncertain terms are we welcomed in the lives of my son, daughter-in-law, or grandchildren. It deeply saddens me that our grandchildren will never know that love we have in our hearts for them. There is just no way to deal with this pain caused from a wound so deeply embedded within my heart. The truth is, I do not feel comfort in the thought of the God and Goddess, and wonder where they are right now.

PARTIALLY CLOAKED, NEVER
FULLY SILENT

by Astarte Moonsilver

I met the Goddess on a warm spring day in 2003 after leaving the Mormon faith.

Of all the Christian-based religions out there, Mormonism is one of the strictest in terms of requirements that need to be fulfilled in order to be deemed worthy of forgiveness for one's sins. And that was the religion of my youth, from thirteen years old until almost thirty-two. I grew up afraid of not measuring up, of not doing enough to ensure my safe passage through the gauntlet of the Sentinel Angels, who would know my every thought and deed and judge me according to my works here on Earth. I was determined to cross the threshold with my family intact, and all the blessings promised to me would be fulfilled. And then, I had the classic epiphany: In the Mormon faith there is a sealing ceremony where you are sealed to your husband and children for all of eternity, even after death. However, it is the husband's decision as to whether or not the children can be sealed to their mother. In the case of divorce, prior to having the children sealed to you, it is still up to the husband who the children are sealed to. My children could not participate in the sacred ordinances because their natural father, whom I had divorced, refused to give his permission for them to be sealed to me in the Mormon temple.

This was very devastating to me, as I had given up almost all worldly desires to obtain this promise; this surety that my children and I would be together in Heaven. I jumped through all the flaming hoops that were laid out for me, and at the final moment, I was told I could not have what I had worked very hard to accomplish. At every step, I had to be interviewed and judged by men who were not even professional trained clergy. The last bishop, of the ward I attended, was a librarian in his mundane life! But, because of the authority of the priesthood bestowed upon all men in Mormonism, I had to subject myself to his approval and his judgment. I intuitively knew that this was not the way a loving, benevolent Creator would treat his/her daughters.

I left Mormonism, after wrestling with the history of polygamous practice within the Mormon belief. Although the mainstream church doesn't practice it anymore, the doctrine has not been removed. It could be reinstated at some future point, when the members become worthy again to practice it. This causes much distress to the women of the religion, and is a common area of dissent among them. I was convinced that no God that I would want to worship would force his daughters to submit to this humiliation and subservient life in order to gain approval and become worthy of acceptance. I resigned from the church in November 2002, not knowing what religious path I would follow, if any at all.

Then I began to research Wicca, in part to protect myself from an individual who had once threatened to use his knowledge of black magic to compel me to love him forever. I wanted to know if it really was a possibility, and how to protect myself. Almost immediately, I discovered that he had no understanding of Wicca, and his claims of power and authority were as hollow as a straw. I learned about the true practice of Wicca and the benevolent nature of the religion, through websites at first. I couldn't believe how many sites there were, and I devoted many hours scouring the pages, lurking and reading. Then, I started buying books. I soon collected over eighty titles, each one more fascinating than the last. But I didn't commit to practicing at first. I just read and savored all the new ideas, and freedom, to discover what I thought most resonated within my spirit.

I felt at peace and knew I was accepted instantly. Sitting in quiet meditation by a lake, I felt a dragonfly land on my arm, and it stayed there for almost a full minute. That was the day that I decided to tell my family that I had chosen my new path. I thought my mother would be happy for me, since she had become convinced that I was an atheist and in danger of eternal damnation for denying God and Mormonism. When I told her that I discovered the Feminine Divine, she actually sort of cowered, like I had just presented her with a snake. She claimed that what I had connected with was evil; that I was being deceived, and that God was, and always will be, male. My sister immediately cracked the wicked-witch jokes, and brought up all the common misconceptions about casting spells and turning people into toads. And she is close to my age, which made it doubly vexing for me to listen to her carry on, as if, she knew all about witches from watching several episodes of *Charmed*.

How sad for them, really. I am grateful to have found Wicca, and I am glad to know the Feminine Divine as our ancient ancestors did for many generations, before the siege of the Hebrew God and the stripping of our feminine identity. I am a Witch. I walk the path of the Old Ones. I am forever learning, evolving, and growing. I will always remember our Mother Goddess.

I wear a pentacle necklace and attend rituals. I've even started a small group here in my hometown, and we observe the Wheel of the Year in cloak-and-dagger fashion. In the future, when my children are grown, I will come blasting out of this broom closet, and open my home to fellow seekers. But, until then, I am forced to keep partially cloaked, although never fully silent.

SERVANT OF BRIGIT, DAUGHTER OF THE FLAME

by Mael Brigde

The third daughter of a large Catholic family, I learned early to consider the well-being of others—kin and stranger—in addition to my own needs and longings, and included those considerations in making decisions in life.

I learned to love deity and its expressions—angels, saints, Mary, Jesus, the Holy Spirit, and God the Father—and to treasure meaningful religious ritual. Turning to deity for inspiration, awe, joy and protection, I imbibed teachings of compassion, justice, integrity, and accountability to God and community. But life was hard, the church offered little help, and I grew angry. A prairie road in a blizzard was the perfect place to ream God out for permitting cruelty, narrow-mindedness, prejudice, and despair, in naked contrast to those teachings. The potency of cold and ice, a muffling cloak of snow, invisibility that offered anonymity and release meters from families cloistered in warm houses—all this made his presence more palpable and personal to me.

God, the elements, nature, justice, rebellion, and over-riding wonder were the fundamental ingredients of my early spiritual formation.

I couldn't ignore injustice. This doesn't mean I couldn't *be* unjust. I learned anger, self-pity, and the myriad confusions we as humans are heir to. But I was never able to completely overlook the effect of my and other's unkind actions, nor was I able to not care.

When I lost patience with the injustices I saw in the church itself, and became dissatisfied with the narrow roles offered women, I began pulling away. This decision was made firm when a priest sermonized about abortion and my sister and I lay in wait to question him. "What if she'd been raped?" we asked when we had him alone. "What if the baby existed because someone had sinned against her?" "It is terrible," he said, "but she must do penance for his transgression, not sin herself."

This dismissal of the woman's perspective was the last straw; I declared myself no longer Catholic. When Jesus freaks came beckoning with their version of peace and love, I listened, but was turned off by a theology that seemed as myopic as what I'd left behind. I became an atheist.

This created an uncomfortable vacuum. When wonderment struck, how could I encompass it? When the world was too much, who should I rail against? When life's passages came and went, how could I mark them? I didn't want to fall back on making the sign of the cross when frightened, or asking God's help when laid low. I needed to tear down the old foundations and build something new, or forever drift back to a set of rituals that meant nothing in my present life, many of which now brought pain and discouragement, rather than hope or peace.

But where could I turn?

I began reading about ancient religions—Greek, Roman, Celtic, African, Old European, indigenous North American, Assyrian, Babylonian, and Sumerian. Their stories moved and inspired me: the wonder of creation, the might and vitality of goddesses and gods who were tied so completely to the Earth and to the lives and sorrows of humanity. I told a friend, "I wish there were still religions that worshipped goddesses." She brought out a book on Wicca and said, "There are."

This began a new and fervent exploration. Starhawk's *The Spiral Dance* taught about the beliefs and rituals of Neo-Pagans. Diane Wolkstein's *Inanna, Queen of Heaven and Earth* offered the poetry of Inanna. Sylvia Brinton Perera's *Descent to the Goddess* drew me to the depths of the soul, in descent to Ereshkigal's underworld.

I began writing prayers to Inanna. Exploring and celebrating the intimacy of the changing seasons through solstices and equinoxes. Feeding my thirst for a better world with the ideals of equality and compassion in women's spirituality. Imbuing myself with ritual.

I found the Goddess, and hungered for more.

With every new experience, each new book, my growing love of earth and her fruits, mythology and its potential to heal the soul, and deities capable of great breadth, enabled me to rebuild my religious framework. I had something to turn to in times of both difficulty and delight.

Then I found Brigit.

I'd read of her, of course. A friend, not himself a Pagan, on seeing my excitement about the Goddess gave me *The Women's Encyclopedia of*

Myths and Secrets. An amazing gateway, it introduced me to countless marvels. I referred to it constantly, until the spine cracked and the Minoan snake goddess on the cover faded and creased.

In that book I found information about an Irish saint who was rooted in a great goddess. Such lovely irony! My terribly Catholic relatives honored a deity that predated Christ. (How grateful I am that they have, or she'd be all but lost.)

My interest sparked, in 1985 I wrote an Amateur Press Association zine about Brigit, saint and goddess. Someone suggested I join Pagan APA, where I befriended Goddess-worshippers. Soon after, I visited St. Brigid's church in Perth, Australia. My connection to her took root and grew. I included Brigit verses in hymns to Inanna, dreamed of a green-haired goddess watching over my bed. I learned to weave rush crosses and cook colcannon, and celebrated her festival with friends and family every year. I combed libraries for references to her and scrawled notes on cards.

Then, in 1993, I did two things that changed my life, giving it a focus and an element of devotion that would strengthen over time. I decided to relight the perpetual flame of Brigit, to share that dedication with other women. And I initiated myself, offering my life to her.

In January, I prepared myself and invited women—Pagan and Christian—to take shifts as Daughters of the Flame. Beginning in Canada, we've had members in many countries—Indonesia, Ireland, England, Bosnia, Australia, New Zealand, Turkey, Greece, Brazil, and the United States. As Brigit's daughters, we are blessed with the charge of keeping her flame alive—in ourselves and in the world. We take part in the exuberant awakening that commitment to her brings.

On Imbolc 1993, I lit her flame, and went with two sisters-in-the-spirit to a glacial mountain stream. I removed my clothes and entered the waters of death, leaving my old self behind. When I emerged, I was clothed in a new garment, and a new consecration. I met the woman channeling the Hag at the streamside:

Mael Brigde: Great Goddess, I am Your daughter, contemplating Your mystery. Grant me entrance into the River of Death, that it may cleanse me and be the Womb of my rebirth.

Hag: In Whose Name do you ask?

Mael Brigde: I ask in the name of the Goddess of Green and Blue and Gold. I ask in Your name, Dark Mother, fire of the Sun, water of the Moon, warrior, gravedigger, mourner. Tender mother, strong daughter, loving sister. Mediator of disputes. I ask in the name of You, the Unbroken Vessel from Whom all life comes and through Whom all is unified.

I ask in the Name of Brigit the Smith, the Morrigan, Whose feet are in the River of Death, Who cleaves flesh from bone, soul from body, in the Name of Brigit the Nourisher and Guide, Danu, Anu, Whose fine hands placed the stepping stones across the stream, in the Name of Brigit the Healer and Consoler, Liberator and Inspirer.

Brigit of the Poets, initiate me. As You loosen the grip of winter, so loosen and liberate me. Breathe life into me this Imbolc as You breathe life into the mouth of the dead winter.

Later, when I had been allowed to pass, had been through the stream and emerged, amazingly warm, on the other side and been welcomed by the Goddess, I was asked to commit myself by the woman channeling the Mother.

Mother: What do you pledge, Daughter?

Mael Brigde: I pledge myself to the fire of life
to the poetry of the soul
to the forging of our strongest,
supplest, most radiant selves
to the healing of my life, ever forward, gently
to the mending of all hurts and conflicts
to the healing of those around me
to the protection and healing of Your living planet
through word and deed and joy.
If I should break faith with you
May the skies fall upon
May the seas drown me
May the earth rise up
and swallow me.

I was unaware of it then, but on Imbolc 1993, when Daughters of the Flame kindled Brigit's fire in Vancouver, Canada, the Catholic Brigidine sisters in Kildare, Ireland, lit it as well. Over the years that followed, numerous groups have sprung up to keep Brigit's flame, and more will emerge. The long darkness is over. Her blaze has reignited.

It's been sixteen years since I kept my first shift. In that time I've met many a woman who is drawn to Brigit, nourished by what she symbolizes and what we can bring forth in offering to the world on her behalf. We've sung songs, written poems, created jewelry and drawings and books. In her name, we have done ritual, performed services of reconciliation and empowerment and compassion. We've sat with the dying, prayed with the suffering, shared our celebrations and our pain, given birth, married, grown discouraged, emerged from heartbreak, and died.

Brigit's daughters have taught me to think carefully about them—when it's easy and when it's difficult. They've inspired me to pick myself up and try again when I feel as though I've failed. They have been tender and grumpy, steady or jumpy, as they go through their lives and I through mine. They've shown courage and love through it all.

The flame of Brigit has been my salvation. The leaves that grow from the wooden altar she placed her hand upon reveal life in my deadened soul. Flames that sprout from the harrow she wore on her head show me purity and grandeur in the humblest person. Her threshold birth teaches of the place that is neither there nor here, but both. She instructed her nuns from the words of a wise madman, took from a king what she needed for her community, gave unstintingly so no being went hungry, with never a shortage in what was left behind.

She brings healing with her waters, illumination from her fire. Her anvil forges a compassionate world. From Brigit comes the lesson that I need to live joyfully on this Earth.

Years ago I wrote to my grade-three teacher, Sister Cecilia, and told her I was no longer a Catholic, but a Pagan. She said she was glad I love nature so much and hoped one day I'd have a relationship with the one who created it.

I smile when I think of this. Many of my hurts around Christianity are healed. I'm reacquainted with Catholics and my childhood faith, and I have rediscovered depth in its stories and ritual. I no longer see Christians as natural enemies—Brigit's generosity played a role there.

Years have passed since my teacher said those words to me. We speak of prayer with each other and there is no illusion that we're praying to the same deity. But we pray for the good of all, and that's enough.

When I sat with the Brigidine Sisters in Kildare, the woman leading the devotion added—"or however we see divinity," with a glance to me—after saying the word "God." I was moved by the grace and gentleness that Brigit's flame can bestow on peoples who have so long been divided from each other.

I thank Brigit for bridging Pagan and Christian worlds. I thank her for being a bridge to myself and to my fellow seekers. Within and without the Pagan and Christian communities, we attend more to our differences than our similarities, and this has brought great harm. Brigit stands above them all, reconciling Protestant and Catholic, Christian and Pagan, atheist and seeker. Her presence is a never-ending blessing in my life.

BORN A WITCH

by Icinia

I was born a Witch. Uh-huh, I was. A great many people will frown on this statement. Some will say it's not possible, that Witches are made, not born. Some will say one cannot be a Witch unless one is initiated into a coven. Well, I'm here to tell you that Witches *are* born, and born Witches *do* lead very productive Witchy lives. Yours truly is living proof.

I was born into an on-again, off-again Catholic family. Sometimes we went to church, sometimes we didn't. It all depended on Dad's mood. If he felt like going, we went; if he didn't, we didn't. Of course, my brothers and I went to Catholic school, where we all shuffled up the hill every first Friday of the month—two by two—to church. We had first communion and confirmation, we listened to the nuns talk about poor starving children and learned about sex education from single, Catholic ladies. Our lives were directed by remote, unsmiling, rigid men who were used to, and, I suspect, delighted in, never being questioned or challenged.

I rejected this religion when I was a very young child. I didn't know it at the time, mostly because I knew we weren't allowed the choice. It was against the rules to question, challenge, or reject. However, during one lecture by the visiting nuns, I had an epiphany. This woman, in her black robes and tight headgear, told us we had to love God, but if we couldn't, it was okay to fear him. That was good enough for me!

Despite everything I was being taught, I *knew*, as far back as memory serves, that I was a Witch. It's curious; I don't know *how* I knew, I just did. We lived out in the middle of nowhere, we had no TV, no magazines, no books. The world was far, far away, undisturbed by the likes of my family. And yet, I knew. I didn't exactly know what Witches did, but I knew it was special and I knew in this way, I was special, too.

Through one thing or another, I wasn't in a position to explore my spiritual side until I was an adult. When I was in my early thirties, I started what I called my Serious Spiritual Quest. The first thing I did was ask questions, especially of very religious people, or people who had a very strong belief in a god. I wanted to know why they believed what they believed, what exactly they got out of going to their worship services on a regular basis. My informal survey produced these results: Some people attended their Christian church because they liked or admired the priest; some people doubted their faith, but continued to go through the motions out of fear or laziness; one person worried about what would happen if, on Judgment Day, she discovered she had been practicing the wrong religion; one person went to Friday night mosque for socializing and the feeling of belonging; one person followed a Buddhist teacher whose philosophy basically said "Don't follow anyone."

On one level I wasn't surprised by the results of my informal survey, because it seemed to me that following a religious or spiritual pathway not of one's own design was an exercise in futility. It must be noted that not a single person told me that they attended their house of worship for the sheer joy of it, or that their spirits were recharged by the service. It seems in these cases that contentment was always just around the corner. On another level, I *was* surprised, specifically at the vigor with which some people pursued their religious life while living with great doubt about their spiritual choice. My little informal survey of friends and family did not produce any *Aha!* moments, but it did reinforce my belief that my rejection of organized religion was the right decision for me.

Inspired by my childhood perception that I was a Witch, my next step was to read everything related to Witchcraft. I read books on Wicca, I read books on what is called the Burning Times, I read books on the Salem Witch trials in America. I read books on goddesses, philosophy, history, and strong women and their accomplishments. I started surfing the Internet. I bought magazines. I read good advice and bad advice, accurate historical presentations and horrible fabrications. At the beginning, I didn't know the difference. However, the more I read, the more I realized that I was not alone. There were other Witches out there! And I wanted to meet them.

So I started taking courses. And it was through these courses that I discovered a wonderful resource center and store, run by incredible people who welcomed me with open arms. The feeling of coming home was overwhelming. I knew the search was over. Not the learning, mind you, but the Serious Spiritual Quest was over. At this point, I knew the rest would be discovery. And so it has been.

I never had to sit anyone down and tell them I was a Witch. I suppose I am lucky in that. Everyone knew, whether they consciously acknowledged the fact or not, that I was a Witch. No one was surprised. No one thought I was crazy. No one hustled their children out of my view. No old ladies fainted, no horses reared nor snorted. It has been a nonissue, really.

I have learned a great deal from other Witches, Wiccans, Odinists, Voodoo and Hoodou practitioners, Druids and many others who consider themselves Pagan. The one common thread is that every single person has been nonjudgmental. Isn't this what it's all about, acceptance? Are we not here to design our own spiritual path?

This is not to say that Paganism is a free-for-all; on the contrary. It is a flowing, living spiritual path that allows one to celebrate the cycle of life, death, and rebirth on one's own terms. It makes sense, doesn't it? We are the architects of our own lives. Why should this not include our spiritual paths? I love this feeling of freedom that permeates everything under the Pagan umbrella. I am here to interact with deities as I see fit, or not. I can call upon the Universe for strength, or not. I can ask my spirit guides for guidance, or not. I can cast a spell any way I want. My altar is set up the way I want it.

I am a Witch. I have always been a Witch. And I love it.

FOREVER A CHRISTIAN WITCH

by Paul Turnbull

"Oh, my Goddess!" she exclaimed. "We've found our herbologist!"

My teacher, and Elder High Priestess, was easy to please. I had made some relatively simple weed identification, and she was ecstatic.

I hadn't yet made my declaration—repeating "I am a Witch" three times—but I was increasingly certain that my many years of growing interest in the feminine aspect of the divine had led me unerringly to Wicca. Along the way, I was also learning about the trees and plants at my home, and a little about their traditional attributes.

My spiritual quest had led me to Christianity, and has never led me away from that faith. But I also found great comfort promised by old European and Celtic religion and folklore. In particular, as a father of five daughters (and four sons), I found myself deeply touched by the power, strength, integration, and beauty expressed by British and Northern European concepts of the Goddess.

Raising daughters led me to challenge my not-so-feminist assumptions. I stayed home with the youngest, and found that I was especially touched by images that would offer her powerful female models and expectations. In trying to keep my mind alive as an at-home dad, and in trying to raise her as a girl who knows her own mind, I saw much of value in this ancient wisdom from Europe.

I believe that certain moments in our lives reach backward and forward in time, in the sense that meaning and imagery can have such a reach. Years ago, I was moved by a Victorian painting of a solitary Witch at her cauldron in a remote outdoor spot. Rather than a bubble-bubble hag, she was portrayed as beautiful, dancer-like, and armed with a sword, or perhaps, a long and sharp wand. The painting is *The Magic Circle* by John William Waterhouse. She is casting a circle, accompanied by a few crows, and is clearly speaking or singing.

A few years later, I attended a Wicca 101 workshop presented by a local High Priestess. Physically, my High Priestess is not especially identical to the woman in Waterhouse's vision. Nor were her ritual robes particularly similar. Yet there she was. As her talk unfolded, I heard the simple facts of Wicca, and of casting a circle to establish safe and sacred space, of the liberty and life inherent in embracing Nature into worship, and the balancing power of recognizing the feminine and the masculine in divinity. I saw, most of all, that Waterhouse had been right.

I know nothing of his thoughts and beliefs, but in that realm where art asserts truth, for me, Waterhouse was right, and I saw it with my own eyes. As presented by this High Priestess, Wicca offered real, not pretended, means for the individual to express the art, beauty, and reality of ritual, including magic, in the here and now.

Soon after I made that classic declaration in my form: "I'm a Christian, and I'm a Witch, I'm a Witch, I'm a Witch!"

I knew that my declaration had been more than sincere. It was real.

Later, other moments led my High Priestess to mutter to me in gentle exasperation, "Oh, Paul, I know that you will always be a Christian, but there is no doubt that you are also a Witch!"

I could answer her with a simple truth: "I know."

WE LOVE ALL LIFE

by Kristen Adams

After the death of my parents, my faith in everything was shattered. I was searching to find out what I believed in or even could believe in. I was a special education teacher and saw children daily who struggled sometimes just to eat and use the restroom. How could this be? How could these things happen?

My husband and I decided to have a child, but I couldn't have children, so a friend said she would carry this baby for us. My husband went to talk to our Christian minister about it and he said, "You need to throw out that whore and the baby that she is carrying, and get your life right with God!" If that was what being a *good* Christian was about, I decided that I no longer wanted any part of it!

Shortly after that, my cousin invited me to go to a class on Wicca. She was very interested in it and didn't want to go alone. I decided to tag along. We walked into a room full of very friendly, loving people and I felt an immediate sense of calm and well being. I sat through the class and realized that Wicca, Paganism, and the like were not about Satanic worship; instead they were about loving nature! It was about loving all the things around us and respecting them, too. What a beautiful concept, and it's the way I choose to live my life anyway.

I sat and spoke with the instructor, and I felt loved and accepted. When he asked me what made me come to class apart from my cousin, I explained that I was told to throw away my baby and her mother, by a Christian minister. He looked at me, took my hands, and said, "We love *all* life!"

From then, I got my hands on everything I could read about Wicca. I took his classes on witchcraft, Tarot, Reiki and whatever else he was teaching. I found a sense of inner peace and a sense of having control of my life for the first time in thirty-three years.

But how was everyone I knew in a mostly Christian society going to deal with my being a Witch? (A title I wear very proudly, by the way.) The first people I told were my husband and my baby's birthmother. Both were accepting, and very loving, and wanted me to share what I had learned. I said to myself, "Okay, this is not so bad!" But I spoke too soon, because when my husband and I told his parents that our new baby would be blessed by a Wiccan High Priest and that there would be no Christening, it did not go over very well. But life went on and they lived with it.

Since then, I have had to come out so many times. My first husband and I grew apart and divorced. When I met my current husband and told him my beliefs, he was completely open to it and has actually studied along with me. In fact, he often asks me for guidance, especially when meditating. When we married, we had a handfasting ceremony. His parents didn't have any idea what that was, but I have learned that sometimes, no matter how proud we are of who we are, we just need to keep other people's feelings and beliefs in mind. When they asked me what a handfasting was, rather than going into the Wiccan beliefs, I simply told them that it was an old Scottish tradition. They accepted that.

We all have different beliefs, ways of worshipping, and ideas about religion. I believe it is a very personal subject, and so everyone should respect each other's beliefs. I simply live my life, and if someone is uncomfortable with who I am or what I believe in, then I have found that I am better off not having them in my life.

The Goddess and the God, the Great Spirit, have shown me a life of calm, peace and happiness. I celebrate my holidays in a way that makes me happy, and my husband and children honor them with me. I thank the Goddess and the God for guiding me in my daily life, and for supporting me through life's tragedies and tough times.

CRAFTY CATALYST: EXPLOITS AND EXITS OF A TEEN WICCAN

by Gwinevere Rain

Sometimes I feel my story is a cliché: a fourteen-year-old female look-ing into Witchcraft after a series of "coincidences" combined with an interest in spells. Yet what started out as a search for magic through the Internet ultimately turned into a genuine desire to find a spiritual path that would nurture me on all levels. Upon researching more thoroughly (and bugging a few witchy web mistresses along the way), I started to learn more about the actual religion of Wicca. This is where my clichéd story ends. Wicca was never a fad to me or some method of rebellion; it was meaningful. After a few short months, I was dedicated literally and figuratively.

Since at fourteen I couldn't keep much to myself, I told my mother and my closest friends. Although everyone was fairly receptive and understanding, there was a certain degree of hesitation. My best friend played with my altar tools without asking. I had to explain that besoms were for cleansing, not riding. Slowly, more people at high school found out. I proudly wore a pentacle around my neck. Because it was high school, there was drama. I was outed in Social Studies class by a fellow student who boldly announced, "Watch out or she'll put a spell on you!"

It was during this same timeframe that the TV show *Charmed* and the movie *The Craft* grew in popularity. Wiccans and Witches were popping up everywhere, like Willow on *Buffy the Vampire Slayer*. This media burst made things simultaneously easier to be Wiccan and harder. Easier because the dialogue was emerging; harder because the supernatural portrayal was at odds with my nature-based religion.

I was a young adult solitary practitioner who mainly used the Internet and books as my resources. I struggled to meet other Wiccans. There were a few Pagan-minded girls at my school, but they didn't take their path as seriously as I took mine. When I inquired about a flyer at a local metaphysical store that I saw for a study group, I was told I wasn't allowed to participate due to my age (even with my mother's consent).

Upon moving to Florida and continuing my solitary practice, I once again turned to the Internet for networking. I started writing for a (now defunct) online magazine which became the catalyst that jumpstarted my writing career. I penned my first book, *Spellcraft for Teens*, when I was sixteen years old. I was thrust into the adult world of publishing and took the final step out of the broom closet. The few family members who didn't know about my Wiccan practice were then aware. I was interviewed on the radio, online, and within various print publications including the popular teen publication, *Seventeen* magazine.

The publishing world may seem glamorous but it is a tough business. Strangers were telling me what to do and how to behave. It was a hectic time and I wasn't prepared for the emotional rollercoaster.

Eventually, I managed to find some balance. I realized that helping my fellow teen Wiccans outweighed any drama. My writing felt more like a mission. Suddenly, I had this platform that enabled me to bring real-life issues to the forefront. I followed up *Spellcraft for Teens* by writing *Moonbeams & Shooting Stars* and *Confessions of a Teenage Witch*. This same calling or mission led me to create my own online magazine specifically dedicated to young-adult practitioners. Throughout the years, *Copper Moon E-zine* has changed formats and publication times, but it has stayed true to its initial goal: to provide a voice for young men and women in their teens and twenties, both novice and seasoned practitioners alike. We are now a weekly publication with author interviews, book and music reviews, Wiccan prayers, and most importantly, essays and articles submitted by our readers.

As a Wiccan starting my tenth year of practice, I believe that connecting with fellow practitioners (through any venue) benefits one's spiritual life. In 2008, I finally found a Pagan community in my area. We meet twice a week outside a coffee shop to form a drum circle and/or chat. Our local metaphysical store is now run by a friend and fellow Pagan whom I met in college three years ago. As I participate in the Pagan community (both locally and globally through the Internet) I keep growing as a Wiccan practitioner and as an individual. I truly believe we all learn from each other. The people that I have met have enriched my life, my path. There is a Pagan song that states, "I am Pagan and I am proud." This lyric holds true in my mind and heart. No matter what obstacles come next, I have faith in myself and in the religion that I so dearly love.

THE MIXED BLESSING OF FOX MEDICINE

by Jeffrey Jarvis

"Are you sowing that salt for a blessing, or for protection? I don't think you'll need the protection here, it's a safe, well-tended park. But I'm sure a blessing for good sales would be useful."

With those few sentences, I made myself known as a practitioner of an alternative spirituality in a very cautious and secretive way. I was at an herb fair in our local state park, and directed my statements to the wife of an artisan blacksmith as she helped set up their booth for demonstrations and sales. Turns out the salt was for both blessing and a border, to keep children from cutting under the rope and getting hurt.

This was in 1988. I'd self-identified as Neo-Pagan for a while by then, having studied whatever texts I could find on mythology, witchcraft, magic and Tarot from the time I was old enough to browse bookstores on my own. I delved through the university libraries in Kent and Akron, mostly pulling up medieval references, with books quoting passages written in Latin and all the arcane and pseudo-scholarly notes and addendums that seemed to hide more than illuminate the meaning of the texts. My spiritual path took in and blended all those studies, and also the time I spent in nature, communing with Spirit all alone. It was always a very solitary path.

I knew how to spot a witch, or a druid, or shaman in the 1960s; they looked more like hippies than anything. So I looked for such people again now that I felt ready to make connections in the community, and tried to find a group that could help me grow in my practice, with little luck. I had no idea how many people who identified as Pagan were living, working, and passing as normal, God-fearing, flag-waving American citizens right under my nose. Just like the blacksmith and his wife.

I felt like a lodge member when I first spoke to them, like my great-grandfather the Freemason, using secret signs and handshakes to say, "Yes, sister, I'm one too. Want to talk?" Over the next few weeks, I visited their place in the farmlands of Wayne County, Ohio. I learned they were each solitaries too, but the people they knew! Artisans, professors, businessmen, writers . . . It was quite some time before I met someone there who fit the stereotype I'd assumed was again the norm.

Making that first connection was a lucky break. They didn't flaunt their spirituality. It seemed that they worked it into their days in such a way that it was present, but if you didn't know to look for it, you'd never notice it at all. And they were often in the public eye, doing craft shows where little old ladies carrying wooden geese and dried flower arrangements walked right up to the booth, not noticing the iron totem pieces mixed in with colonial reproduction candle holders and plant hooks. If these two could walk a Pagan path in public without calling unwanted attention to themselves, why couldn't I?

At work sometimes I'd wear a little pewter pentacle designed to look as if it were shaped of wood and leaves. Whenever people did notice it and mention it to me, it was always without fail assumed to be a Star of David. Either people didn't understand the difference between a five and six pointed star, or their minds glossed it into something with which they had at least some familiarity—another example of hiding in plain sight. So coming out to the general public was pretty much a nonevent for me.

When I started attending SCA meetings and going to Renaissance faires, I met people who recognized the symbolism and presented themselves as Pagan. Once again, other than the habit of dressing in fantastical costume at the events, most of these people were quite normal in appearance. And they led me, after a few years of medieval camping, to my first full-blown Pagan festival. This was another sort of coming out.

It was at those festivals every year in July that I started trying to integrate myself into the Pagan community. Having successfully learned to walk in the everyday world without being singled out or even noticed, I now had to teach myself how to stand out. Because there in the fields and woods, bumping shoulders with famous (or maybe infamous) elders and fixtures of the Neo-Pagan subculture, I might as well have been invisible.

Making connections in the alternative spirituality community was for me much more difficult than being a Pagan on the street. As a solitary and not associated with any particular path or lineage or teacher, there was nothing about me that stood out. Going gray, having been around just long enough, and doing pretty accurate Tarot readings helped me to fit in somewhat, and eventually I gained the notice of some elders. Still to this day, though, when I sit around a campfire with any of them, or go with them to an event, I don't stand out at all. I might as well be a rocky exo-planet around a distant star. I'm just not noticeable at all.

So my ability to blend in and become invisible, what for the lack of a better description I'll call "fox medicine," is a mixed blessing. In the everyday, with my parents or neighbors or coworkers, I'm just myself and not anything strange at all. The spiritual path I walk, my beliefs, my practices are there and just not noticed. But with fellow Pagans, my invisibility has probably kept me from making connections that could help me grow, or perhaps better be able to make an effective contribution to the community.

Were I to have done anything differently, I might have tried to find a different way to put myself forward, to become a more visible part of the Pagan community. But just by virtue of watching at the side of influential people, I've learned much of the dynamics of various Pagan groups. And by walking the walk as I have, I'm sure there are things I have to share.

Sometimes, you have to not be so concerned how much you might stand out. I may never walk down Main Street in a flowing velvet cloak and wizard hat. But I wouldn't be afraid of scattering a little salt.

WALKING A STRANGE YET FAMILIAR SPIRITUAL PATH

by John David Hickey

I grew up in the suburbs of Quebec City in the 1970s, raised by Catholic parents who were not very religious people. In those days, the schools were heavily influenced by religious bodies, which meant you went to either a Catholic or Protestant school. I went to the English Catholic elementary and high school, which included religious instruction in the curriculum.

As a young lad, I took my religious duties very seriously. I went to church faithfully every Sunday with my family. I often served as an altar boy, tending to the sacred duties during mass. When I was able to get to church under my own power (riding my bicycle), my parent stopped attending church (although my mother sometimes attended a francophone church closer to home). I believed in living a good life and doing the right thing, as was taught to us by our priests and encouraged by my community.

However, if you are expecting to hear horror stories of abuse and corruption perpetrated by my Catholic religious leaders, which led me to a life of Paganism as a form of rebellion against my oppressors, I'm afraid I must disappoint you. The priests in my Catholic church, who worked with the school as well as their own congregation, were good, honorable men who served their community faithfully. It was by their example, and by the example set by my family and community, that formed the foundation of my own morality.

When I left home to attend the *Université de Sherbrooke* in the Eastern Townships, I did briefly look for another church to attend Sunday services. I quickly realized that the pleasure I took in attending church had more to do with that community of people than the liturgy of the Word of God.

As I grew older, I found I had serious issues with the Catholic Church and its position on sexuality, men's issues, women's issues, and its politics. I decided that the Catholic Church itself was corrupt, but that the religion it represented was still valid for me. I would be Christian, but not Catholic.

And yet, as I met more and more people from a variety of cultures and religious backgrounds, I felt myself drifting farther and farther away from my Christian identity. I felt in my soul that there was a God, but that the nature of that God had to be more than what I had been taught. It made no sense to me that God, who was a being so beyond imagination, the embodiment of such perfection and omnipotence, could suffer from such human emotions and failings such as jealousy, anger, and even vengeance as was described in the Catholic Bible.

At that point, I decided that, although I had a need for spiritual expression, the Christian model did not meet my needs, nor did it reflect my values. I found some spiritual solace in the poetry I wrote and I felt a strong spiritual connection to something greater than myself when I acted in local community plays. I felt that creating art was a way for me to express the spiritual side of myself, although I still felt like something was missing.

Then in the mid-1990s, I met a woman that I dated for a couple of months who was Wiccan. I had no idea what a Wiccan was, much less what a Pagan was, but she patiently answered my questions and lent me a few of her books (I devoured Cunningham's *Wicca for the Solitary Practitioner* within hours).

I was fascinated by the concept of gender balance in the Divine. It made much more sense to me that the gods could be male and female, and although they had different responsibilities, they were equal in power and presence.

The magical traditions were also familiar, much more personal, and made me feel much more connected to a Divine presence that was described as being inherent in all things rather than ever-apart from us. Catholics understand the power of symbol, ritual, and community, so making the transition from being a passive ritual witness to an active participant was not only easy and exciting, it seemed completely natural.

Like many people who discover Paganism, I felt a strong sense of coming home. Simply scratching the philosophical surface of Wicca revealed truths and concepts that I had already concluded in my own spiritual wanderings. Here was a community of people who felt an undercurrent of connection to the earth and sky, to the sun and moon, and to each other in a way that was not abstract or ethereal, but present in the here and now.

So it turns out I wasn't crazy after all. But now, what could I do with this new-found spiritual awakening?

Over the next few years, I kept this personal enlightenment mostly to myself. I tried to talk about to a couple of friends, but their initial reaction to it ranged from amusement, confusion, and even deep concern for my mental well-being. I learned quickly to keep the subject to myself and do my own research. I read published books on the subject of Paganism, and surfed my way through a few early websites that featured spinning pentacles and smiling dragons and unicorns. Some of the concepts they presented were interesting, but a lot of it seemed like fluff and window-dressing. Many times I wondered if I had traded a fire-and-brimstone God for a free-loving hippie God who seemed to be content living in the Goddess's basement and her shadow.

Then in the spring of 1999, I decided that it was time to meet these people in the flesh. I found a Pagan e-list that included events taking place in the Montreal area, I chatted with a few people online, making introductions and connections, and committed myself to attending my first public Beltane ritual.

To be honest, I don't remember much about that first ritual. I remember the studio was at top of a narrow staircase, I remember being warmly welcomed by the priest who had organized the ritual, and being reassured that everything would be fine and I didn't need to be so nervous. I was terrified: not because I feared for my immortal soul, but because I didn't want to say or do the wrong thing.

I didn't understand the symbols, the jargon, or the gestures of the ritual, and yet it still felt right. I could feel a sense of connection to something that still eluded me during that ritual, but I felt closer to it than ever before.

As the years passed, I attended more and more public rituals. I took classes on Wicca and Paganism, met more like-minded folks, and made strong connections with a multitude of Pagans from all sorts of traditions, philosophies, and geographical locations. I have expanded my own spiritual development from conversations, debates, and experiences with these people than from any book or website.

In 2001, I started volunteering my time at the Montreal Pagan Resource Centre, which is a drop-in center for people who are looking for information about Paganism or alternative spirituality. I've been president of the MPRC since 2005, and we are still serving the needs of our Pagan community as best we can.

And yes, I have met many crazy, unhinged people in that time, too. And even they, in their own mad path, have taught me about the dangers and pitfalls that are inherent in Pagan belief and philosophy. They have taught me that it is critical to keep a firm foothold in the rigors of reality, while expanding my understanding of the unknowable. Maintaining a balance between these worlds is a life-long challenge, but the exercise will keep you grounded and allow you to ever-question the knowledge that comes your way.

I am fairly open about my Pagan beliefs and it really hasn't had a negative impact on me in any way. As a Pagan, I have been interviewed by the local newspaper and I have been interviewed on the radio and television. Most people who discover that I am Pagan are more curious than fearful or hostile. In Montreal, we are blessed to live in such an open-minded city that does not suffer from extreme religious or ethnic intolerance.

When I choose to hide my Pagan beliefs, I do so because I don't want to make others uncomfortable or I don't want to draw undue attention to myself. My spiritual path is very personal to me, and although I don't mind providing information to others who ask about it, I don't enjoy being mocked or antagonized about it.

Paganism has provided me with a deeper understanding of the nature of Divinity, the strength of community, and the peace of living harmoniously. Being an active Pagan in my community has introduced me to some of the most amazing people I have ever met and has allowed me to find common ground upon which we could share our lives, loves, and spiritual growth.

The Pagan path is not an easy path to walk; anyone who comes to Paganism looking for answers will end up with even more questions. But it is in exploring those questions than we can add new layers of meaning to our lives, and in doing so, enrich those lives around us.

THE PLACE I CALL HOME

by Idril Rogers

I admit that I was a rebel as a kid. I played with the Ouija board, read all sorts of books that my parents said were totally inappropriate for a young Catholic girl growing up in England, and I always wore black clothes, which my father hated. To me, it all just felt right.

In my twenties and thirties, I suffered badly from depression and overdosed on drugs more than once. It was a very difficult and painful time for me, but I finally turned the corner in my forties. I finally found what I had been looking for! I was surfing the Net one day looking into Paganism. I started to research and the more I read the more I wanted to read. The more I learned the more I searched for more. It was all starting to make sense. Herbs had always fascinated me and I cooked with any that I could find. I had also always been drawn to crystals. I already owned quite a collection, but I didn't know why. I never had normal perfume either, but instead I was more interested in the heavy oils that I found in the weird shops around the city. I have always been in touch with the Wiccan side of myself, but I just didn't know it. Finally, everything was starting to fall into place. I had found the Goddess! She was the one thing that was missing all my life! I now know that she had been there all along, but I hadn't opened my eyes long enough to see her. I studied hard and became a Witch.

Years later I met my husband. He was from Wiltshire, England. The first time he took me back to his home county, something stirred inside me, and I knew this was where I was supposed to be. Here I was, in the most mystical place in England! He took me around to see the sights, the magical white horses, Stonehenge, and Avebury Stone Circle. That's when it all hit me and I had the most amazing feeling of belonging, Avebury was my true spiritual home. The calmness that took me over was like nothing I had ever experienced before in my life — the warmth of the stones, the love of the Goddess. It was all there.

It took me no time at all to decide to pack up our house in the midlands, but I had to explain to my family that I was moving down south. My three daughters were all very supportive. They knew about my spiritual beliefs and were happy for me that I had found my missing link. Now my parents, well, they were a different kettle of fish. Mom was in her nineties and Dad was in his late seventies at the time. So for me to leave was a big deal in and of its own, but at the same time for them to find out that their baby was a witch!

I sat down with them and told them all about the feelings I had hidden for years and about the sadness that ruled my life. I told them about the feeling deep in my heart, the happiness and inner peace I had found since learning about Wicca.

Mom just shook her head in disappointment. Dad thought it was just a phase that I would grow out of. He never did want me to grow up and have ideas of my own. He just wanted me to be his little girl forever. In the end, I think I allayed their fears and helped them to understand me better.

Today, I have no regrets about moving because here in the southwest of England there is a far better acceptance of Pagans than there was back in the midlands. People are quite used to seeing others walking around in cloaks and holding staffs. They don't bat an eyelid. The Goddess found me and here I found her. My life has changed beyond recognition and I am happier than I can ever remember! My depression has become something I can easily deal with. I simply talk to the Goddess every day and she helps me take the right steps that lead me along the path I was born to walk. Today a besom hangs in my lounge, pentagrams adorn my walls, I wear a pentagram to protect myself, and I pray to the Goddess every day. Today, with the Goddess in my life, I feel whole and complete.

MY SAVIOR

by Bonnie S. Hann

As a child, my family and I went to a Methodist Church. It was okay, but nothing spectacular by any means. What I most remember enjoying about it was that at the age of twelve or thirteen I was asked to help out with the younger kids and sometimes substituted for the Sunday School teacher.

My mother and father divorced when I was fourteen. My dad was abusive toward me my whole life. This turned me into an angry and rebellious teenager. Mom remarried an older man who demanded respect. Jim believed that he was the man of the house and that my mother's first obligation should be to him. One summer day, my stepfather actually came after me and was going to beat me for something I had done. I yelled, "If you think you're fucking big enough then go ahead!" Then I ran up a hill, sat on a picnic table, and watched our house from there. He never did come out after me. I was having a really hard time believing in God then. I was forced to attend church every Sunday with people who spoke in tongues and who tried to make everyone feel guilty and uncomfortable for being a sinner, but

I knew that day that some external force in my life was protecting me. I was just unable to put my finger on it. I knew though, that there was no way that I was going to go forward in church to accept Jesus Christ as my savior. Where the hell was he all the times I was beaten by my father as my mother just stood and watched it happen? Where the hell was he when my stepfather seemed to be following in my father's footsteps?

Shortly after they married, my mother and stepfather kicked me out of the house, and I lost all hope and faith in God. I lived in a one bedroom apartment that was infested with bugs, and dated an abusive guy. I was severely depressed and as I listened to the noises in the night, I became terrified and wondered how long it would take for someone to find me if I had died. I was sick and hungry and only had about fifteen or sixteen dollars a week for food.

Then I met Scott! He was the most interesting and intriguing man I had ever met. Things began to change right before my very eyes. He said he could read my mind, and he had an incredible way about him. He kept insisting that everything was going to be okay and when I asked him how he knew that he said, "I just know, and that is enough." I found myself angered by him. Here I was in the depths of despair and hopelessness and he was always so even and calm. He said he was a Witch. I was fascinated and wanted to learn more about him and what being a Witch meant. I wanted the inner stillness and knowing that he had. So, he began to teach me. We worshipped together and it was amazing! Wicca fit the answers to my questions perfectly. What an eye-opening experience learning all of this was! I felt the Goddess's arms envelop me and I was safe and comfortable for the first time in my life. There was no question in my mind that I too, was a Witch!

I have found that for the very first time in my life, my faith has brought bigger and better things for me including Scott (now my husband) and our children, and our wonderful home. The people where I live in Pennsylvania believe Witches are evil and Satanic. Even my own sister believes that Witches and Satanists are one and the same and refuses to talk to me about my faith. My biological father learned about my faith just recently when the children, Scott, and I made the trip to Massachusetts for my Wiccan group's annual Samhain ritual. I told my father about the ritual, and how I had seen my husband's deceased father walking to join us through the trees in the surrounding woods. The howling wind and pelting rain did not prevent him from joining and celebrating with us. I told my dad that I had an incredible experience there in Massachusetts and it helped affirm my beliefs once again. He said, "It's not that witchcraft stuff is it?" "Well, not what you might think, Dad." "Okay, so long as it's not that witchcraft stuff," he replied. I chuckled under my breath and thought that it was good enough that I said it and he knows. My mother and stepfather are going to be another story. They will probably flip out and want to pray for me to be saved. But I know that it won't be long before I tell them. I never felt this way in my life, and I am proud of it. They will have to know because I just can't keep it bottled inside anymore. I cannot deny it. I am a Witch!

Becoming a Green Witch

by Janice Mathieson Wright

I sometimes joke that I "married into" Paganism. My husband is Pagan, and when we were first dating I would sometimes gently ask about his personal practices, and he'd explain as much as he could about his spirituality. At the time, I was reading the *Tao Te Ching* in search of a spiritual path that suited me. But Taoism didn't "take" with me. It's a beautiful philosophy, but I couldn't figure out how to build any kind of spiritual practice around it, and that's what I was looking for: a personal spiritual practice that resonated with my life, my values, and, for lack of a better word, my beliefs.

Since my husband and many of his close friends were Pagan, and it was supposedly a nature-based religion, and the natural world was a big part of my personal spirituality, I started to poke at Paganism, mainly by reading books, websites, and e-lists. I've always found it much easier to learn things by reading books than by asking people questions (probably because I'm an introvert), and I didn't really know what questions to ask.

The biggest barrier that I kept hitting as I read introductory-level Pagan material was the emphasis on deity. What I was reading kept telling me how empowered I now was as a woman, because as a Pagan I believed in the Goddess (and possibly also the God). The focus on the female aspect of deity seemed to be so central to Paganism that it *excluded* me. To put it crudely, I don't "believe in" the Goddess and the God. But it has nothing to do with "belief;" I'm certainly not about to deny that the God and the Goddess (or Hecate, or Diana, or Pan, or Jesus, or Mohammed) *exist* in some way. It's just that my concept of deity is something that is pure energy, and exists primarily on the spiritual plane. The idea of deity having very human attributes like personality quirks and gender doesn't make much sense to me. And it certainly doesn't fit into my personal spirituality. What I was reading was telling me that if I didn't "believe in" or at least "work with" the Goddess and the God, then I couldn't be a Pagan. So I left it for a while.

Tarot is an important part of my husband's spiritual practice, and one day we had a long conversation about it. His explanations confirmed for me that Tarot was, at very least, a great tool for accessing one's own subconscious mind, and possibly a lot more besides. I eventually bought the World Spirit Tarot for myself and started to work with my deck by drawing a card first thing in the morning. I soon figured out that the Tarot work went much, much better if I did that centering and grounding thing that I'd read about in the Paganism 101 books. Every day I recorded what I was discovering about Tarot (and about myself, naturally) in a nice notebook. Without having made any kind of decision to do so, the centering and grounding gradually evolved into meditation, and then into meditation and energy work.

So I was doing daily grounding and centering, meditation and energy work, and Tarot draw, and recording it all in my special notebook. But I wasn't calling myself a Pagan because of that pesky Goddess. To be fair, it wasn't just the Goddess and other deities. Heck, if it was I probably would have just called myself an "atheist Pagan" and jumped right in! It was also the fact that much of the introductory material I found was somewhat Wicca-centric (or otherwise Gardner-derived), and so tended toward, "Here's how to practice witchcraft: You need a pentacle, and an image of the Goddess, and an athame, and a wand, and here's how you arrange them on your altar, and here's how to cast a circle, and here's how to celebrate the Sabbats."

And most of this stuff, though interesting, didn't resonate with me. Having a pretty ceremonial knife that you were supposed to never cut anything with seems slightly bizarre to someone who has spent most of her adult life with a Swiss Army knife in her pocket. Knives are meant to cut things: that's their function, their purpose. My way of seeing and interacting with the natural world (which is what my spirituality is all about) seemed to simply not mesh with the descriptions of Paganism that I was finding.

Then I read *The Way of the Green Witch*, which essentially said that I didn't need to work with gods or goddesses unless I felt like it, no formal ritual was required, an essential tool was a good sharp knife with which to cut things, and that worship could be as simple as hoeing the garden. It also said a lot of other stuff about earth energies, gardening, cooking, and crafting, most of which resonated strongly with me in a way that none of the other material I had read had.

And I thought, "That's it! That's me! I'm a hoeing the garden kind of Pagan!"

Now I had a starting point that felt right, and I could begin to develop my personal spiritual practice as a green witch.

My current practice is rooted in the deep connection I feel to the land. I walk in the fields and woods behind my house every day. I'm getting to know every tree, learning where the outcrops of bedrock are, where the water pools after it rains, and discovering what species of shrubs and grasses grow where. I notice how high the geese are flying and in which direction and in groups of how many. I'm feeling the seasons change, and sensing the patterns and flows of the natural energies of this little patch of the earth that is mine to love and protect and cherish and nurture. I try to learn all I can about the local flora and fauna. I have a shelf of reference books on things like trees, birds, wildflowers, herbs, and edible wild plants, and whenever I notice something new I try to look it up, figure out what it is, and remember its name. For me the first step in learning about the spiritual or magical properties of a plant, animal, or tree is to understand as much as I can about its physical nature, its habitat, and so on. Then I try to learn about its spiritual or magical nature through working with it or observing it or meditating on it or connecting with its energy.

As a green witch, my day-to-day life and my Pagan path aren't separate: they're one and the same. I don't treat my natural surroundings as something so sacred that I shouldn't touch them. There are wild apple trees in our hedgerow that I would like to rehabilitate if possible. This means they need a fairly severe pruning, and that I will have to cut down the buckthorn shrubs that are competing with the apple trees for food, water, and light. I'm cutting saplings out of our hedgerow to use as tomato stakes: it makes more sense to me than buying tomato stakes from a garden center. More saplings will grow.

My long-term goal is to produce as much of our own food as possible here on our land. This spring I'm planting a large organic vegetable garden, getting a flock of heritage-breed chickens for both eggs and meat, and planting fruit and nut trees using the principals of permaculture. I choose heritage varieties of plants and animals that were developed before modern farming methods because they are more ecologically sound choices. Plus they taste better.

We try to buy most of what we can't grow ourselves from the farmer's market, because we like knowing where our food comes from. As author Michael Pollan puts it, we "shake the hand that feeds us." Our beef comes from our friend Peter's farm, where we've stood in the middle of his field and petted his Belted Galloway cows. We buy red deer and wild boar sausages and free range eggs from Hans, and pork, lamb and our Christmas turkey from Artje. The vegetables that I can't grow myself, I buy from Alan. We get apples and juice from Tessa. Our flour, beans, cooking oil, and dog food comes from the organic mill that's been in Tom's family for three generations. We also like the fact that our money is going directly to our neighbors, not to the shareholders of a big corporation. My personal focus on ecologically sound living and homesteading isn't necessarily Pagan. But it's all part of my path because that's the way I *live* my path.

The green witch path is a solitary one by nature (no pun intended), but one of my biggest challenges is not having anyone to discuss my path with, most of the time. Practicing alone, you tend to get bogged down and stuck in a rut after a while, and you need new ideas or a fresh perspective or a reality check from someone else to help you get unstuck. Part of the problem is, of course, living out here in a rural area. When I lived in Montreal I worked regularly with the Montreal Reclaiming community, and I got a lot out of it. I would love to have one or two people nearby whose paths are similar to my own, to share ideas with. I know there must be people reasonably local to me who follow a similar path, the difficulty is finding them. I was recently at an organic farming conference that was attended by over four hundred people. Chances are that a few of them were Pagans, but of course I had no way of identifying them, or them me. We're starting to network with Pagans in our local community, however, so hopefully I will be able to meet a few people to have these sorts of discussions with. The closest I tend to get these days is discussing tomato varieties with Alan at the farmer's market.

One of the best ways to find people with similar paths who work with or talk to and exchange ideas with is, of course, through the larger Pagan community. Unfortunately I still sometimes feel excluded, like I did when I started reading introductory Paganism books. Because my path is quite different from mainstream Paganism (I don't celebrate the Sabbats, or cast a circle to do magic, or work with gods and goddesses), it's kind of alienating to hear from people in "my" spiritual community that "as Pagans we do *this*," and have *this* be something totally foreign to my spirituality or my practice.

The core of my practice is the land and my connection to it. Terry Pratchett describes it beautifully in his novel *A Hat Full of Sky*: "She tells the land what it is, and it tells her who she is."

Having been out here in our new home for only half a year, I'm still bonding with the land. I'm looking forward to working with it more, getting to know it better, and shaping it into a sustainable homestead. With any luck that's something I will continue to work on for the rest of my life.

I'm also very aware of the fact that where I'm going could well change. The more I practice, read, learn, and experience, the more I understand what certain authors have said or why certain things tend to be done a certain way. Things that I don't currently find useful might some day turn out to be so. Things that don't resonate with me now may some day. The universe is very good at reminding you that you may have chosen a path, but you're not in charge of what you'll find as you walk along it.

CELEBRATING THE SEASONS:
CHRISTIANS AND PAGANS

by Joan Withington

I was born on November 1, 1950; Samhain in the Witch community. My parents were devout Roman Catholics. My mother had an
Irish ancestry, and Dad had been an altar boy. I attended St. Joseph's
Church and school, going through the usual rites of passage for a
Catholic girl of the time, which included first communion, confession, confirmation, benediction on Sunday afternoons, and, of
course, mass daily.

There are a number of things from that time that I have carried
with me into my life as a Wiccan, such as a fondness for the Wiccan
Wheel of the Year. It is similar to the church celebrating seasons. Christmas began on the first Sunday of Advent as we lit candles each week to
bring us nearer to the big day. The Christmas festivities were centered
on the birth of Jesus, not on Santa or present giving. Although we did
receive gifts, this was never the first thing associated with Christmas.
Carols were sung with gusto and the Christmas season ended with
the Three Wise Men visiting on January 6. Only then did decorations
come down, as Twelfth Night held just as much importance as Decem-

ber 25. New Year's Day was the feast of the Circumcision, so New Year's Eve, rather than being a night of celebration, was a day of fasting and abstinence.

With spring came Easter and brand new clothes, and, of course, Easter eggs! Though the weeks before had been hard with Lenten fasts and constant reminders of suffering and crucifixion, the following months were filled with various Saint's feasts and Holy Days, which all make up the Catholic Wheel of the Year. My favorite was May, with the crowning of Mary as the Queen of the May with a circlet of flowers. Very Pagan indeed!

Running parallel with all of this was the natural wheel of the year. My Dad had a small holding, which we called the garden, on which he grew vegetables, flowers, and even two grapevines. So I grew up with the planting season, growing season, and harvest followed by the winter's rest. My memories of the plot of land are my happy days. I would follow Dad around with my small watering can, weeding and planting, then watching the plants grow. We had a well from which we drew water for the plants. It was always dark and frightening to me, and it had a funny smell because the water from it was hardly the purest in the world! The river that ran at the bottom of the garden, the local river Douglas, stank with the overflow from the many factories and mills in town at the time. Its color varied from green to bright orange, depending on what dye they were using that day. On Mondays it was frequently covered in white suds, from many a dolly tub used to wash clothes, and sometimes children, emptied into it on wash day!

In our garden, I remember a black current orchard that had grown so dense that the center could only be accessed by crawling under the brambles to the middle where it opened up so you could stand. This was my hideaway. This was the place where I met the fairy folk. I played with them happily for hours in that small space. I was an only child, you see, and by accident of geography and time (just after World War II), there were no more children in the area. So, I played happily alone with only the friends that I could see.

As I grew into my teens, like so many others, I began to question my religious upbringing. The only stability for me was the Blessed Virgin. I know now this was the Goddess speaking to me; Isis in another incarnation; Diana still great among the Ephesians. But at this time, I still didn't hear her voice.

In the background, the papers exposed the scandal of Witchcraft in the suburbs, and a man by the name of Alex Saunders and his wife, Maxine, had brought the Craft into the light of the media. I felt drawn to read about these strange rituals taking place in people's homes and on open heathland. But, I still felt the old fears of Devil worship—Satanism. I also remembered stories of Denis Wheatley and selling one's soul to the Devil.

Over time, I found my psychic abilities becoming stronger by the week and I remember my first astral projection one very warm sunny day. I remember seeing symbols and rune stones. At this time they meant nothing to me, but the occult world was calling. I stopped being frightened by things others called the occult and I read more and more, discovering that magic was neither good nor evil. I obtained rare books for that time, like the *Key of Solomon*, which is easily available on the Internet today. Its mysteries drew me to read about the craft. I read *What Witches Do* by Stewart Farrar. Unbeknown to me at the time, mention of my future High Priestess (Helen from Lancashire) lay within its pages.

I joined a paranormal investigation group operating in the Preston area, where I heard a male Witch speak of the Craft with such reverence. I hadn't heard anything like that since I had last gone to High Mass. He talked about the elements as living spirits. It took me right back to my childhood in the black current orchard when I played with fairy spirits.

I bought a book called *Buckland's Complete Book of Witchcraft*. This book changed my views on the Craft over night. Gone was my fear and doubt! I knew I was finally on the right track. I gained an understanding of the God and Goddess and their roles in the Wheel of the Year that had been such a big a part of my early life. Things now made sense.

I heard a little voice inside of me say, "I'll show you the way."

The following month I received my copy of *The Wiccan* through the post. On the back cover I noticed an ad that read, "Gardnerian/Traditional Coven seeks members. Merseyside Area." Well, Merseyside to me meant Liverpool, which is not that far from where I lived, so I replied to the address given. To my surprise, the address was Tyne and Wear. This is at the other side of the country. I wrote them anyway because I was curious and a month later I got a reply for Plymouth, on the south coast of England! The High Priestess wanted to know my history, what I had read, etc. So I wrote a long essay and posted it back to her. A couple of weeks later she wrote back to me asking to meet. The shock is she lived just fifteen minutes from my house. She was a school teacher and had to keep a very low profile, hence the cloak-and-dagger contact.

I learned a lot from Helen, and I owe her even more. Without her I would not be where I am now. My life revolves around the Craft; its festivals, moon esbats, initiations, and of course, teaching the newbies.

Sadly my children did not follow me into the Craft, but that is their path. They all know what I do, as does all my family. My mother is very elderly now, and has never accepted what I do, but has let me be. My son-in-law jokes, "Men call their mothers-in-law witches and I can boast that mine really is one!"

Am I out of the broom closet? Oh yes! We have appeared on TV, radio, and the newspapers. Yes, I am out! I believe that being out of the broom closet can be both good and bad. Being out makes it is easier for seekers to find their way and the shelves of bookstores are stuffed with books on the subject. The downfall to that is that today it is so easy to go into a bookshop and take a book off the shelf, read a few chapters, and *hey presto*, I'm a Witch! It is too easy today to be trapped by the glamour, the illusion, the public face, the strange clothes, and the pentacles hanging from every orifice. It would seem that getting through the glamour is today's challenge. It is not easy to find a good teacher within a coven grove group, but it is important to learn first-hand from someone who had trod the path before you. I am so glad that I had that experience and couldn't imagine my life without the Goddess in it.

FOUR EPIPHANIES

by Brendan Myers

Let me tell you a tale of four spiritual discoveries, each built on the foundation of the last, each leading to the revelation of the next. And let us start this tale when I was a boy in the little village of Elora, which I still consider my hometown.

In my free hours after school or on weekends when I had no responsibilities, I would ride my bicycle all over every street in my village, to explore it everywhere, to know it intimately, and to claim it as my own. I knew the streets by the shape of the cracks and potholes. I knew the houses by the friendly and unfriendly dogs that would bark at my passing. I knew the bushes where wild raspberries grew. In the winter I knew the shapes of the snow drifts, and the best toboggan hills, and I knew spring was coming when the cedar trees threw off the snow that covered their boughs. There was a conservation area to the west of the village. It started at the place where the Grand River cut a deep gorge through the limestone, and it went on forever. I knew this terrain as intimately as I knew the streets and tracks and parks of the village itself. I knew the sinkholes and shallow caves where I could hide, together with a stash of pebbles to throw at passing tourists. I knew how to race through the trees at top speed without crashing into the crags and steppes. I knew the overlooks and plateaus where I could watch the beaten paths, unseen. I invented names for those places, and stories of battles and romances and escapes from danger that happened there. And I had a regular route that took me to each one, in its sequence, like a sentry on guard. These were my sacred places, and this was my land.

Something about this knowledge struck me as *spiritual*, even before I knew the meaning of the word. I attended a good Catholic school, and I went to church on Sundays. I made a good show of being devout, since I knew it would please the adults around me. I was never popular among my classmates, and never much interested in the things that interested them. Indeed I was one of the runts of the playground. In this way I lived in the school and the church and the family home like everyone else. But my forest of cedar trees and limestone cliffs was where I really lived.

My first spiritual discovery was the forest. It was not that there was always something new every time I explored it. Nor did I feel a magical calling to be among the trees and waters. It was not that my forest was pristine and untouched. Indeed campsites, paved roads, water wells, stone walls, and other signs of human management could be found everywhere. Yet I think that I knew, somewhere in my childhood mind, that when I set out on my bicycle, and ran my regular path from one secret place to the next, and saw that all was in order, I was most truly *myself*. What is more, when I raced through the trees on the riverside at full speed, or when I scaled the cliffs of the gorge with my bare hands, or did any number of reckless things with no thought of injury or death, on those days I knew that I was *strong*.

That was my life. But that was another life, for it was a lifetime ago. I am no longer a child, and my town is no longer a village. Like other people, I eventually discovered rebellion, and beer, and sex. Somewhere here I also discovered *mythology*. My father taught Irish mythology to my sisters and me as bedtime tales when we were children. It was perhaps his way of preserving his connectedness to the country where he was born. So when I was in high school, and a friend gave me a copy of *The Book of Druidry* by Ross Nichols, I felt on familiar ground. I learned that ancient druids built their sacred groves in deep forests. Well, I had a forest practically next door, and I was already using its sacred groves. The Druid, Celtic model of a holy man, changed from a historical curiosity into a real possibility. Where once the Irish myths were only a collection of stories about my father's country, they became serious accounts of how people met with the great immensities of life and death. Here were stories of heroes traveling to the otherworld, returning with gifts from the gods. Here were heroes confronting their destiny and accomplishing greatness, but for one tragic flaw, which brought them death. Real human lives are just the same. Mythology offered me a way to recover and preserve that sense of strength that I remembered from my childhood adventuring. I became an activist in the environmental movement, and then in the labor movement: the activist seemed to me the modern form of the old Celtic warrior.

At a Celtic music festival I met a red-haired woman who played the Irish harp and spoke in soft tones about magic. She brought me to a campground where about fifty people gathered for the weekend. Some were clothed in flowers and green leaves, some in the furs and horns of animals; some painted spirals and strange symbols on their skin. They spoke of the world and the events in their lives with the same language of mythology that excited me so much. I was introduced to a text called *The Charge of the Goddess* by Doreen Valiente. Although it is not a Druidic text, I still think it the very finest expression of spiritual identity written by anyone, anywhere, in the whole of the twentieth century. As these people described her, the Goddess is a mother, a healer and a caregiver, a sexual partner, a controller of the fertility of plants and the soil, a king-maker and a sponsor of chieftains and warriors, a controller of fate and destiny, a teacher, a fighter, and a witch. Someone who commits herself to the culture of the goddess can be any of those things, and more. For She lives in the bodies, hearts, and minds of all women and men. She reveals herself to us through the beautiful things in the natural world, and in human relationships. She has no laws and commandments, but dancing, singing, feasting, making music, and love. At our festival, we made a man from stalks of new corn, and proclaimed him our King. We gave him gifts and sang him songs from the wood to thank him for the harvest. Then we cut off his head and burned his body in a fire. And we baked bread with some of his ashes and declared him restored to life. Each evening we feasted on beef and pork and venison, and drank homemade wine from huge drinking-horns, and sang bawdy songs of high summer green. We returned to our tents, two by two, when the fire burned low, but not to sleep—not yet, dear love, not yet to sleep. And we called this scandalous behavior a religion! It was another world altogether. And it was the good life—my third spiritual discovery.

For many years that, too, was my life. But other forces have initiated other changes in me since those heady days in the Clann of the Moon. I discovered that I was a rotten actor, and therefore didn't belong in a university drama program. I experienced love both true and unrequited; I endured loneliness; and I witnessed death. Serious questions were burning in my head, and the stock answers of my teachers and friends were no longer good enough. Somewhere in this mess I discovered *philosophy*. I think I was energized for philosophy by the astonishing proposition that we can solve every problem we know with the courageous use of human intelligence. What mythology does with symbol and narrative storytelling, philosophy does with systematic reason. And this is no less a spiritual thing. We can achieve illumination and release by means of our own will and effort, both independently and together with friends—without assistance from anything supernatural, without churches, without institutions, without need for the saving grace of God.

Philosophy consists in the exploration of four comprehensive questions: What is Goodness? What is Reality? What is Truth? and, What is Beauty? You already know these questions. As a child you posed them to your parents when you said "Why should I?" and "How do you know?" and "What's going on?" No one can escape these questions, unless he consigns himself to ignorance, and to all the troubles that come with it. Actually, someone who does engage these questions is not guaranteed an escape from ignorance. Yet such a person is offered a chance to meet the immensities of life and death in an honest and forthright way. There is no better source of knowledge, no better foundation for a worthwhile life, than the intellectual examination of ultimate questions in dialogue with the Earth, with one's friends and lovers, with one's innermost loneliness, and one's coming death. Indeed in classical and medieval philosophy *Reason* was said to be the very presence of God within the human soul. By means of reason, a human being could get inside the mind of God, and obtain an experience of eternity. Philosophy is a spiritual thing. I consider this the fourth and most significant of my spiritual discoveries.

Philosophy quelled my interest in ritual. But as if in compensation, it gave me a new way to understand the role of the Druid. Almost every written historical source that describes ancient Druids says that they were the philosophers of the Celtic people. They were as good as the Greeks at mathematics and oratory. They taught that the soul is immortal and is reborn elsewhere after death. They taught a few moral doctrines too: especially heroic virtue concepts like honor, courage, generosity, friendship, and justice. As a professional philosopher, I felt I could serve my community in much the same way that ancient Druids served theirs. And like them, I studied nature. I took up doctoral studies in Europe, on a good scholarship, and I studied environmental ethics. I trekked the wind-battered west coast of Ireland, the meadows and hedgerows of England, and the tree-thick hills of middle Germany, in search of new thoughts. I visited the original locations of the mythologies that I knew so well: Emhain Macha, Glastonbury, Newgrange, Knock na Rae, the Hill of Tara. It was an exciting time for me. Somewhere among those days I both invented and discovered a theory of ethics that I named The Call of the Immensity. I published it in my third book, and it has guided my life ever since.

These four discoveries together seem to me the ingredients of a consistent and satisfying spiritual life. Proper pride can be found when one knows and lives close to one's land. Narrative storytelling and mythology renders the world inhabitable. Philosophical questioning and intellectual acumen, which everyone has a talent for, can be a source of enlightenment. And whatever things are empowering, pleasurable, and loving — these are sacred. These are the teachings that lift us up, and render our lives meaningful, magical, and *worth* the long troubled while. Our modern society, dominated as it often is by malaise, apathy, injustice, cynicism, fear, and loneliness, needs to hear this kind of message.

THANKS TO MY DAUGHTER

by Brenda Gibson

My first experience with Wicca was about three years ago. I had moved from my hometown in Ohio to Massachusetts. Shortly after moving, I flew back to Ohio to visit my family. My daughter had become involved in something called Wicca and had joined a coven. I had no idea what Wicca was, and you can imagine the picture that I had in my mind of a coven. I envisioned a group of black-cloaked women, sitting around a cauldron, casting spells. Okay, the cauldron might be stretching it a bit, but it still sounded very dark and mysterious to me.

During my visit, my daughter took me to a Summer Solstice ritual. Again, I had no clue! Even though I was a forty-six-year-old woman at the time, I was still up for anything. What I remember most about that ritual had absolutely no meaning for me at the time. It was held in a large field on a warm summer's day under a bright, cloudless sky. A gathering of witches in the daytime and out in the open was quite a surprise for me. But I figured they knew what they were doing. There were about thirty women and men, which I thought a little odd; men couldn't be witches, could they? Not one person, including the woman that I assumed was the leader, was wearing a dark cloak. I was somewhat disappointed, but still very curious. She did have very long, dark, straight hair and was dressed in what I would call *funky clothing*. There was a small table in front of her where candles, incense, tree branches, pinecones, and flowers were copiously displayed. I also saw what appeared to be a wand.

We formed a circle and were instructed to turn in each direction as the leader held her wand aloft and spoke in a strong voice. She called out to no one, at least, not that I could see. Following her lead, I turned in each direction with the rest of the group, and repeated words at the appropriate times. When she finished speaking, we all joined hands and began singing. Now, this was more like it! My blood began to flow and I started to feel alive. We danced around the circle slowly at first, and then faster and faster, until we were huddled tightly together while still holding hands. Then, we reversed directions and I realized that we were back to the original circle, but actually beside different people, and still holding hands. How that had happened is still a mystery to me. Everyone was out of breath, sweating, and smiling, or laughing. I was so confused. I thought this was supposed to be a very somber affair. It soon quieted down.

The leader then began walking around the inside of the circle, stopping at each person, asking us to speak our names and write a wish on an index card. She then collected them. At the time, I didn't realize we were performing magic. Magic, to me, meant casting spells in secret. I kept waiting for what I defined as magic, but it didn't happen.

Then another woman began singing in a beautiful voice without any music. The words were beyond me. I looked across the circle at my daughter and had no idea why suddenly I was flooded with so much emotion, that tears were streaming down my cheeks. My daughter just smiled at me.

The leader instructed us to turn and face the different directions, just as we had done at the beginning of the ritual. Again, she spoke to no one that I could see. The ritual was now over.

After our circle broke up, my daughter and I got into our car and followed the procession to an old bookstore where a feast awaited us. We sat on the floor eating, talking, and laughing. I suddenly realized that I had just participated in my first Wiccan ritual and just knew that this was the first of many more to come. I was excited and my mind was reeling with so many questions. I didn't know what had happened to me in that field, but a warm, peaceful feeling had washed over me. My daughter explained as much as she could and I learned later that you can't really teach anyone about Wicca, the Craft, or spirituality, because it's up to each individual to learn on her own when she is ready.

I returned home with the book *Spiral Dance* by Starhawk. I consider myself a fairly intelligent person, but *Spiral Dance* was way over my head. So I put it aside, still finding myself thinking about Wicca and wondering what it was actually all about. That's when the coincidence happened.

A couple of weeks later, my daughter sent me a list of Wiccan stores in my area. There was one in a nearby town. My sense of direction leaves a lot to be desired, and I was fairly new to the area, so I figured I would never find it. It just so happens though, that I was out of work at the time and had an appointment with the unemployment office located in the same town. I knew I'd probably get lost and never find the store, so I didn't plan on looking for it. But I still kept the list in my car just in case I changed my mind.

After driving around the buildings of an industrial park a couple of times, I finally found the unemployment office. I parked my car, looked up, and right beside it was the very store I wanted to look for. A chill ran down my spine. It really shook me. Was this a coincidence or was I for some unknown reason meant to find it?

When my appointment at the unemployment office ended, I walked over to the store and made my way in cautiously. I didn't know what to expect, but I was greeted warmly by the owner. As we began talking a little about Wicca, I noticed all of the strange items on the shelves and what looked like a small library. Very soft music played in the background and I felt very comfortable in that store. I took it all in and walked out a couple of hours later with two Wiccan books by Scott Cunningham for beginning solitary practitioners. And so my journey continues.

ARE YOU WICCAN?

by Sandi Dunham

I have been Pagan all of my life, but the road to figure that out has not been short or smooth. Both of my grandparents passed away when I was young and rumor has it that one of them was a Scottish Witch, but unfortunately, I was raised a Lutheran. I say it was unfortunate because I had loads of questions, most of which made the pastor very unhappy. Truth be known, I was there for the answers, but I felt that the church was keeping the truth from me and I wanted to know why. The teachings were incomplete and I just wanted to know who really wrote the Bible. I asked about Adam and Eve with skepticism, but to no avail. All I got for an answer was, "You are not reading the Bible the way it was meant to be understood." Well, how did they know that?

So, off I went on my merry way searching for something more. While searching, I decided that maybe the answer was in the Jewish faith. I mean after all, they started the whole Christian thing. But I only found more disappointment there because they are just as bound to the Torah as the Christians are to the Bible. They aren't even allowed to write out the word *God*.

I was having such a difficult time because I saw deity as a many-faceted gem; no matter how you looked at its many faces, it was still the same gem. So, I decided to go my own way, and I found myself greeting the morning with a blessing, "Thank you for allowing me to wake this morning and for bringing me blessings throughout my day." I strived to be the best person I could be and tried really hard not to hurt anyone. I always ended my day with the following prayer, "Thank you for helping me through the day and watch over me tonight so that I may see another." At that point in my life I was resigned to the fact that I just wasn't going to find my answers.

I was very interested in Tarot and divination as a teen, but I was told that under no uncertain circumstances was I ever to play with the Devil's tools in my mother's home. So I studied them on my own and left my parents out of it. It's funny that when people don't understand something or are afraid of it, it just becomes evil and wrong; they are not willing to open their minds and instead they just forbid it.

I studied several other religions for a while too, but none of them touched my soul. None of them could explain why I could feel other people's pain and how I could also hear their thoughts. I kept quiet about all of this though, because it scares people and I didn't want people to be afraid of me.

That was until I shared some of these thoughts and feelings with an online group I belonged to. I was thirty at the time and one day when we were talking, one of the girls in the group asked me, "Are you Wiccan?"

"Wiccan? What the heck is that?" I asked.

She explained that from listening to what I was saying, she just had to ask. I told her I had no idea what was she talking about. When she explained it to me, I told her that I had been taught my entire life to believe that Witchcraft was evil and the Devil's work, so I never would have looked into that. Needless to say, that conversation made me so curious that I began looking into Wicca. Wow, what an eye-opening experience! The answers were right on the pages of the books that I read. Someone actually did have my answers. I read so much and I compared it to what I felt inside. It was like the doors and windows blew wide open. So much made sense to me. I found myself saying, "Thank goodness that there are others that see things the way I do. I am not a freak or weird." I was overtaken by such a feeling of calm and peace. It was such an amazing revelation to know that what I was, who I was, was just different than most, but it was real and I was not all alone.

After this incredible discovery in my life, I was faced with a challenging decision. Did I want to practice solitary or in a coven? Neither one of these choices really tickled me. Covens seemed to be almost as bad as organized religion; each saying that their way was the only way, and solitary practice was not working for me either. I am too social for that. I had been spiritually alone for far too long.

I decided to look for an open Pagan group in my area and found a multitradition Pagan group that had much of what I was looking for. During my time with them, I researched, studied, and learned while also raising my children as Wiccans. I did not want to hide what I believed in and I wanted my children to be proud of who and what they were, too. We became so active in this group and it had become such a part of our lives that I knew I had to tell my family and friends. I was really stressed about it, though. I was afraid that everyone I knew would think I was evil, or that I was going to hurt them. I knew that they all had preconceived ideas about what Wicca and Witchcraft were.

My best friend took the news better than I could have expected; in fact, she confirmed that I was just being me. Another friend completely freaked and expressed concern for my soul because, after all, she knew I would end up in hell. I am still working to help her understand because we have been friends for too long to just walk away. My mother said that I can do whatever I want, so long as I am not practicing any Devil worship in her home, and my sister said, "I always knew you were a Witch," and she didn't mean in a Wiccan kind of way. Interestingly enough, my in-laws found out by accident. They showed up at my home uninvited and unannounced, so I had no time to hide my books and my altar like I always do when I am expecting them. When my mother-in-law saw my stuff she started asking questions. Strangely, she seemed sincerely interested in it. So we talked openly and she seemed okay.

Today I belong to a Wiccan congregation called Trinity Temple in Albany, New York. When they opened their doors we went as a family. My son and daughter learn about the ways of the Craft right beside me. We have a wonderfully eclectic group that has so much to offer and it is heartwarming to worship with a group of like-minded people along with my children.

MY OWN PATH

by Rob St. Martin

My path is difficult to describe. When pressed to compartmentalize it, I say I follow a self-defined path of eclectic Celtic shamanism, but it's more than that: there's some chaos magic, some Buddhism, some of this and some of that. Fox is my totem; my spirituality encompasses many paths. I spent a long time coming to my Paganism, or at least, admitting it to myself. I did a lot of research on the way, picking and choosing the elements that made the most sense to me.

I was baptized and raised Catholic, but it never resonated within me. Though I went to Catholic school, my religion classes were just another class; the few times we went to church were family affairs I had little choice in. I was confirmed, but that was a choice I made to please my parents, not through any commitment to Christianity. History classes in high school pointed out the glaring hypocrisies that led to the Crusades, the Inquisition, the witch hunts, the Holocaust. After high school, Christianity and I parted ways with very little ceremony, but it was several years before I fully embraced Paganism.

Over those years I gathered around me a supportive group of friends, which I'd now call my circle. But then we were just four like-minded individuals who felt a deep connection to each other, to nature, and to our growing spirituality. Our souls had connected in a way none of us could describe, beyond saying that we must have known each other in our past lives. We would get together once a month, making dinner as a group, spending an evening in each other's company, talking about spirituality and belief and faith and all that big meaningful stuff that was setting the stage for my self-initiation. I find it somewhat ironic (or maybe not, considering) that I fully embraced my Paganism and self-initiated on a weekend when every other member of my not-quite-a-circle was out of town and unreachable.

It was my first time casting a circle. First time working any kind of magic. First time in a self-induced meditative trance. It was intense and extremely emotional. I was casting off my past, rejecting my upbringing. I embraced a path, a faith, a belief system, that I had created myself, from the bits and pieces of my own research into the world's religions—bits and pieces that resonated within me, that spoke to my soul. No external validation. No practices hallowed by tradition and consecrated by time. Just me, alone, working it out myself. Looking to books for guidance, but ultimately, making my own choices, finding my own way. It was terrifying and exhilarating.

That sense of empowerment kept me going for days, weeks. Even now, a decade later, I can feel its echoes. I had touched something greater than myself, seen through the looking glass, experienced a power, a majesty, that I'd never once felt in church. I shared my experience with my not-quite-a-circle, but it was still mine, no one else's. And I could travel to that place, recapture that feeling, whenever I wanted, at my own pace, learning on my own time, at my own speed. No priest telling me what to do or I would be judged. No teacher grading me on my conformity and regurgitation.

Time and distance played its inevitable role and the not-quite-a-circle parted ways. We remained friends, but it wasn't the same, and I found myself completely alone on my path, working my own magic, travelling on my own spirit quests. I did my own research, and spoke to a variety of other like-minded individuals, expanding my understanding, seeking new experiences. I never hid my alternative spirituality from my non-Pagan friends, but I didn't make a point of telling them, either. It wasn't something I felt needed to be spoken aloud, needed to be advertised. I'm not a very private person—ask me about myself and there's very little I won't tell you—but this seemed to be something I needed to keep to myself. It wasn't until years later, after I'd been to my first fest, that I made an announcement on my LiveJournal, to everyone I knew—and many people I didn't—clearly outlining my beliefs.

Reactions were pretty much as expected. My Pagan and Pagan-friendly friends were supportive and encouraging, and if anyone else wasn't, they kept it to themselves. My Pagan spirituality has made me some amazing friends, people I might not have met otherwise. I've gone to festivals and public rituals. It's even helped my writing career: I've contributed to a local alternative spirituality magazine, both fiction and nonfiction articles, and it's led to sales of my books at fests. Meet-

ing and getting to know other Pagan writers has led to good friendships with kindred spirits.

Coming out to my family was somewhat more difficult. My mother
is the most devoutly Catholic of us; my father is largely agnostic. My
brother asked a few questions but is quietly supportive. Of the three,
telling my father was the most difficult. My mother just wanted to
know if I still celebrated Christmas (I do), but my dad wanted to know
why I had chosen Paganism. Of all the questions I anticipated, that was
not even in the top twenty. I explained to him that I couldn't live in a
universe that didn't contain magic, and wonder, and personal enlightenment. He seemed doubtful, but that's pretty much what I expected.
Telling them was difficult, each for different reasons, but ultimately
boiled down to not wanting to disappoint them. Their opinions had
shaped my upbringing, and pleasing them had always been a priority
to me. Knowing that my chosen path might upset or displease them
kept me from telling them for years; although I did tell them before
I announced it online.

I doubt that most of the rest of my family know, though I haven't
exactly hidden my religious affiliation on Facebook. If they asked, I'd
no longer be as cautious about telling them, as I once might have been.
Once a secret is out, it's easier to repeat. That said, I don't go out of
my way to tell people, because my spirituality is mine. I've followed a
solitary path for a decade now, although I did spend a year in an informal, actual, circle; a wonderful experience but ultimately, not for me.
It's given me so very much that no one can take away. And it's a path
I made myself.

WHO I REALLY AM

by *Deirdre Anne Hebert*

"You don't have to be like everyone else. Just be yourself." These words still resound in my mind from when I first heard them and I suppose they always will.

I grew up in a small city in southeastern New Hampshire, in a very conservative Catholic family. The men in my family were soldiers and I was expected to follow suit. Both of my grandfathers fought in World War I, and I have one uncle who was a Marine, and another who was a Green Beret. In my family, men were men and Memorial Day was an important family holiday.

Duty and ritual both came to be an important part of my life at an early age, but beneath all of this was deep-seated pain. This pain was a constant reminder that I wasn't who I was being told to be. Somehow, I knew that I wasn't a boy, but instead that I was really a girl. This was something that my family wasn't equipped to deal with. Though they tried their best to help me, back in the 1960s *gender dysphoria* (as the condition is known in psychological terms) wasn't understood, especially not in small towns.

My parents' treatment consisted of what today might be called immersion therapy. I was called to be an altar boy and made to play baseball and other sports. At Catholic school, the playgrounds were segregated and a fence separated the boys from the girls.

At one point, I wrote my parents a letter explaining my feeling of being trapped in a body of the wrong sex. My parents blew up and threatened to send me to the state mental hospital. I later heard from a local priest that such thoughts were quite evil and unless I repented I might go to hell. So for many years I didn't speak to anyone about my feelings and tried to live as I thought God would want me to. I followed in the footsteps of the men in my family and joined the military.

My first assignment in the Air Force was at North Truro Air Force Station in Massachusetts, just south of Provincetown, which is a rather famous LGBT (Lesbian–Gay–Bisexual–Transgender) vacation spot. While I didn't act then on my gender dysphoria, I learned something about it: I wasn't alone. I also, unfortunately, in not wanting to deal with who I really was, took refuge in drugs and alcohol. It seemed to me that if I wasn't able to be myself, then an acceptable solution would be to shut off my feelings. In 1982, while still in North Truro, a poem came to me. I wasn't sure how it came to me, but today I believe that it channeled through me. This poem gave me a deep sense of what it felt like to be a woman and more specifically, a Witch. I didn't have any real understanding of what a Witch was when I wrote it, but the woman's feelings in that poem were all too familiar to me. I began to find out what I could about female-based spirituality, and eventually found Starhawk. By the 1980s, books on Paganism were becoming a bit easier to find. I read quite a few, but still couldn't break the idea that there was something wrong with me.

I continued to do what I thought was right, thinking that if I was just a good enough Christian, that God would change me and I would accept his plan for me. I went through periods of reading about the God and Goddess and then renouncing that by burning books and striving to be a good Christian. Eventually, I met a woman, or rather, she met me. As a music minister active in my church, I was in the public eye. She saw me and took an interest. I was thinking that maybe this was God's sign, a way to bring about that change in me. We eventually became engaged and by the time we were married she knew that I didn't always like to wear men's clothes. I suppose that she thought it might be a quirk that would eventually go away.

Needless to say, after the romance was over, things got rocky. Looking back at all of the pain I endured internally during those years as I struggled with who I really was, I still would not have changed a thing. My wife and I had two children together, and I'm incredibly thankful for both of my daughters.

Eventually though, my wife recognized that I wasn't going to change who I was and that she was not going to be able to accept it for the rest of her life. We went to counseling and a very wise therapist remarked, "There are times when two people have completely different viewpoints, and both are right." I came to understand that I couldn't be who someone else wanted me to be, and I couldn't make her change her mind about what she wanted either.

While I was learning to accept the truth about myself, I found that I was still lacking coping mechanisms. I became depressed and suicidal. Shortly after that, I was diagnosed with bipolar disorder and spent the next four years in and out of mental institutions. I had some remarkable teachers during this time. One remarkable woman who did a Tarot spread for me said, "I see a man and a woman, and they are both you." I later came to understand that this High Priestess was also a transsexual and had worked with people like me before. I hope to meet her again someday because she and I had been through such similar experiences. To this day, I continue to learn from what she taught me.

As time went on, I found that alcohol and helplessness were my god and goddess. Waking up in intensive care one afternoon, I knew that something needed to change. Someone in a support group asked me, "Do you think you've had enough?" I knew that I had. I needed to finally, once and for all, understand that I couldn't be anyone else. I needed to be who I was, so I wrote a creed.

For those of you who grew up Catholic, you'll likely know that creeds begin with the words "I believe." The creed I wrote literally changed my life! Some people use creeds as teaching tools, for rote memorization to learn what a group believes. My creed helped me to understand what I already know: That being transsexual gives me a relationship with the God and Goddess that no one else could ever understand. It's helped me to be myself because I can't live in stealth-mode as a transsexual or a Wiccan. I need to be open. To hide, to be in the closet, is in essence to admit that there is something wrong with who or what I am. When I allow myself to believe that there is something wrong with me, I put myself in a dangerous position and begin to feed the engine of self-hatred that almost destroyed me in the past. For this reason, I live a public life as both a transsexual and a Wiccan. This requires that I know what I truly believe. When someone sees my pentacle and wishes to engage me in a conversation about why Satanism is wrong and Jesus is better, I don't run away, but instead look at it as an opportunity to educate them about what I really believe. They often find that it is quite different from what they think it is or from what they have been taught.

Through all of this, I have also learned that it is important to give back to the world, even if you think you haven't gotten what you deserve from it. I am here, I have a place to live, clothes on my back, food to eat, and people to love. I have no reason to be stingy. The God and Goddess do provide. So in giving back, recently, I began to host one of the few live Pagan radio programs that I know of and I'm working with others to start a LGBT (Lesbian-Gay-Bisexual-Transgender) telephone hotline that will provide a telephone point of contact. Each person on the phone will have a huge list of resources including: churches that are LGBT friendly, civil-union information, referrals to groups that handle sexual assault, homeless shelters, and more.

Today it is safe to say that the words "Just be yourself" and they still echo in my mind, although I am certain that my parents and many others in this world would rather that I be who they want me to be. But only in embracing my faith and giving back to this world have I found sanity and true health.

WHEN THE FAIRE CAME TO TOWN

by Mary Lavoie

It's always interesting when your husband outs you to another parent at the local elementary school. It's also interesting when the reaction is, "Wicca? What's that?" And your husband says, "You know, she's a Witch."

My mother asked the same thing when she commented on my pretty necklace. She asked, "Is that the Star of David?" "No, Mom, it's a pentacle. You see, I've been studying Wicca for some time now." She questioned, "Wicca? What's that?" I'm still not sure that she understood when I answered, "You know, Mom, I'm a Witch."

My mom always tried to do the right thing for her children. I went to Catholic school when I was a child and made my first communion at St. Margaret's Church. I was later confirmed in my early twenties at a different church, St. Mary's. I was her youngest child, so she was able to spend more time with me because my siblings were all much older. Every summer she would take me to the city for wonderful trips through the old homes, historic sites, and funky little shops. We lived in Beverly, Massachusetts, just over the line from Salem. What a wonderful way to start my journey!

Of course, there were always television shows like *Bewitched* and *I Dream of Jeannie,* too. I even got Agnes Moorehead's autograph and some memorabilia when the cast of *Bewitched* came to Salem to film several of their shows. Little did I know at the time that I was a Witch in training. Even at such a young age, I was always searching for a spiritual connection. The Catholic Church was a wonderful place, but somehow something was just missing. I always prayed to the Blessed Mother instead of Jesus. She was my first sacred Divine feminine connection. I just didn't know it at the time.

I never lost my love for Salem. I spent so much time there connecting with something, but I just didn't know what. I loved to visit Laurie Cabot's shop and even had my cards read with her. I would have given anything to have taken one of Laurie Cabot's classes, but in the late 1970s and early 1980s Wicca and Witchcraft were still very much taboo. At least they were in this Catholic girl's mind I met a wonderful man, Jerry, who became my husband in 1987. We got married on October 31. Shortly after we were married, we bought a condo in Salem where we began our family. Although Jerry had no particular spiritual path at that time, he bought me my first and only beautiful crystal ball with a pewter stand and my first Tarot deck. At the time I thought he was crazy. They were the coolest gifts I had ever received from anyone, but considering my upbringing, well, let's just say that I was still very leery of these types of things.

When Jerry and I had children, I took over my Mom's routine and began bringing them on wonderful walks through old Salem. It was so beautiful connecting with the ancient trees along the brick sidewalks while wondering what it was like back then. We also enjoyed family trips back to the Renaissance times at King Richard's Faire.

Eventually, we moved to a little town in southern Maine. At the time, something was gnawing at me and I felt it necessary to teach my children about Christianity. We attended the local Congregational Church and I dragged my husband along the entire time. Jerry and I had numerous discussions about spirituality and organized religion throughout the years of our marriage and we never did see eye to eye on the subject. He felt that whatever the Higher Power was, it certainly couldn't only accept Christians in the hereafter. He questioned, "What about the Buddhists, Jews, Native Americans, and people from all other religions for that matter? They can't possibly be excluded from heaven or whatever was actually out there."

As time passed, and my oldest child, Tanya, grew into a beautiful young teen, she became interested in all the same things I did at her age. She was my buddy on road trips to Salem, where we toured the home of Rebecca Nurse and took long walks through the old cemeteries. She was outgoing and vibrant; so much more than I ever was.

Then, my entire life changed when the Maine Renaissance Faire came to town. It was amazing! They built an entire town within our town, deep in the heart of the Maine woods. Although admittedly a smaller version than the King Richard's Faire, it was just as wonderful. In some ways it was even more spectacular. Tanya loved it so much she began volunteering in the café as a serving wench. That's all it took. Our lives have never been the same.

I'll never forget the day after volunteering for weeks at the Faire, Tanya came home and asked if it was okay for her to start learning about Wicca. "Mom, the owner of the faire is a Witch and she offered to teach me!" What an inspiration that woman turned out to be for my daughter and also for me. They were the nicest people ever and more than willing to share their knowledge. They invited us to full moon rituals and showed us the way to the Divine Spirit, teaching us about the gods and goddesses and how to embody Wicca as a way of life. I learned that it was just me and the goddess. The freedom I felt in my heart was just amazing.

Well, the rest is history. It took my daughter's strength and conviction to pull me out of the broom closet and to lead me down the path that I had always been searching for. And, what a wonderfully rich and beautiful path it is. My daughter Tanya has been my inspiration. She had the courage and strength to open her heart, her mind, and her spirit to embrace her warrior Goddess within. Had it not been for her, I would still be searching.

An Unexpected Awakening

by Toni Peebles Franks

It isn't easy to step off the beaten path in the buckle of the Bible belt. My father is a Baptist minister, so I grew up in a very strict Baptist household. As a child, I wasn't allowed to wear shorts or makeup. My family went to church three times a week. There were countless revivals, Watch Night services, vacation Bible schools, Sunday dinners on the grounds, and Friday night singings. I had to attend them all, and believe it or not, I was a true believer in all of it. I didn't question any part of it. I just wanted to be sure that I had truly taken all the steps I needed to, in order to be saved. Looking back at it now, however, I do remember finding it amusing to see all of the different colors radiating from the people in church. Back then, I didn't know what an aura was, so I just figured that everyone could see them. Often I would look at the iridescent colors around people's bodies and I had a strange knowing about what kind of mood they were in. Brown was depressed or sick, green was alive, yellow happy, orange full of energy and unable to sit still. This was my life until I was twenty, but then I began to question things and took time to learn about different religious beliefs. I actually found it refreshing to combine spirituality with acceptance of others. During this time of spiritual awakening, I learned about Wicca, but found I was just too confused about life in general to settle on any one thing. I let circumstances take me where they would. I soon came to realize that something was missing from my life.

Then one day my daughter mentioned the Devil. I immediately knew it was time to rethink our family's approach to spiritual education. I finally just allowed myself and my children to stop going to church all together. I told myself I would "home church." My husband and I are hardly typical Alabamians anyway. My children have been taught by us from their earliest memories that God is the same everywhere; people just call him different names, and some people are happier thinking of God as a She. My children's catchphrase, from the time they could talk, was "we are all connected in the circle of life." It was a quote from *The Lion King*, a Disney movie. They have always known that sometimes girls marry girls and boys marry boys, because that's just how God made them. Once, at the age of six, my daughter started to pass by a tree, and stopped to give it a gentle pat and a smile.

That's when the dreams started. I began to acknowledge to myself that I was indeed on a Pagan path, it just felt so perfect a fit for me, but I began to have vivid dreams about my children being in danger. Sometimes the imagery would be obvious, like when I dreamed that they were swimming in murky water filled with snakes that they couldn't see, but that I knew were there. Other times, the dreams were more subtle, like the one where my mother was trying to get my daughter to teach Sunday school at her church. These dreams made me panic and I began to feel so uneasy. It was one thing for me to endanger my own soul to eternal brimstone, but quite another for me to take my children with me. It's scary enough declaring myself as a spiritual searcher, and it's scary enough just being a Mom, but admitting to myself that I was Pagan and allowing my children to see me hold stones to balance my chakras? What was I thinking! What was I doing?

It wasn't easy for me by any means, but I embraced my true beliefs and started slowly. I had faith in the God and Goddess to guide me and my children to what was right! At first, I began to leave my books about Wicca and Witchcraft on the coffee table, instead of hiding them away so my children wouldn't see them. Then I began to openly read the Tarot cards for my closest friends. I taught my children about stones; how they were very old and had lots of divine energy in them, and that we could use that energy to heal ourselves and others. I gave my children opals and topaz to prevent them from having bad dreams. I showed them my runes and taught them about how to combine the runes with some herbs from the garden in order to make things happen. They often hear me chant my spells, like the one I used when I desperately wanted my pumpkin plants to grow: "Pumpkins, Pumpkins grow for me, you will be cherished, you will see. As I will! So mote it be!"

The dreams have all gone away now. I have peace in showing them my path and also in allowing them to go to church with their Daddy, who has chosen to remain Christian. They are old enough now to understand that people find God in many different ways, and that it is best to leave everyone's spirituality up to them. Only they can decide what they feel in their hearts. So now when my children see me outside with my candles, lifting my arms up, throwing my head back and saying rhyming couplets, they just say to one another, "Mom's praying again," and sometimes they even join me!

For the Love of My Community

by Amanda Hyde

When I was asked to write about my discovery of Paganism, I assumed it would be a simple thing to do. I mean, who knows my history better than I? What I found, though, is that one's discovery of a spiritual path is anything but simple. It has many facets to it, it touches every area of a person's life and it evolves constantly.

To prod my memory, I began reading through the journals I have kept over the years and the one theme I found to be fairly consistent was my passion for organizing events and bringing our community together.

One of the interesting pieces of my history is that prior to walking a Pagan path, between the ages of eight and eighteen, I was an active Jehovah's Witness. This upbringing played a large though indirect part in the direction I have taken today.

I spent many years giving talks on stage and preaching door-to-door. As a result, I became skilled in public speaking, researching, and organization; I also gained confidence and an ability to keep calm in the face of conflict. These are all skills that I continue to use as I walk my Pagan path and as I organize various events in the community.

My upbringing is also one of the major reasons why I believe I turned to Paganism. It was a direct result of my urge to be rebellious, and not due to my desire for a new spiritual path. I wanted to become a person utterly different than the innocent girl who had left Moncton, New Brunswick. I didn't consider Wicca as a way of life, I was simply into it and I wore a pentacle because it represented the opposite of everything I had been brought up to believe.

My initial exposure to Paganism took place in Halifax, Nova Scotia, in 1997. I was eighteen and had left home to go to college. My two years in Halifax were life changing in many ways. I was living independently for the first time and one of the first things I chose to do when I moved was to stop attending church. I just wanted to enjoy myself and have a good time. During the first six months, I avoided anything related to religion. Having spent ten years within an extremely strict faith, I wanted nothing to do with it.

It was during this time that I came across Little Mysteries, a Pagan shop in the heart of downtown. It caught my eye initially because it represented an area of spirituality that was so different from everything I knew about religion. I spent a long time during my first visit, perusing the merchandise and, although I remained too shy to ask any questions, I left with a couple of books, some stones and an ankh. The interest I had came and went in waves for a number of months, but soon I had a craving for a deeper understanding of my existence and my role in this world.

I loved school while growing up and since graduating I have continued to take courses simply to satisfy my need for knowledge and understanding. Toward the end of my college program I realized that I needed to have more depth in my life beyond simply partying, going clubbing, attending college, and preparing for a future career. My boyfriend at the time would sit with me over coffee and we would discuss our existence, our purpose, and various philosophical theories. I have always been an overly analytical person and I slowly realized through these conversations that, although I had backed away from religion, I continued to believe that there was something out there larger than myself, something Divine.

The one experience that truly jumpstarted my reading and studying Paganism was when our professor organized a field trip to the Shambala Buddhist Centre for a meditation class. She meant for us to gain a new perspective on handling stress. I gained a new perspective on my life, how I fit in this world, and how powerful our energy and our minds are. I left the mediation class and spent that evening reading through the books I had purchased.

I moved to Ontario in 1999, where my reading and studying continued in earnest. I read the two books I had purchased from cover to cover a few times and I started to apply their suggestions regarding meditations and working with the elements.

Slowly, I began to see how Paganism could fill the areas of my life that I had swept aside. I had an aversion to religious structure and one of the biggest attractions for me within Paganism was that I could maintain total control over my practice. I could meditate when

I wanted, cast a circle or not; there was no one looking over my shoulder, telling me what to do and when to do it.

From 2000 to 2003 I worked at a Pagan shop called Mystasia, which had stores in both Burlington and Hamilton, Ontario. This regular exposure to Paganism helped me internalize my practice. My beliefs became a part of my life, not a hobby to be shelved until I had time, and it was at that time that I finally became a true Pagan. That process also aided me greatly in my job as I met customers who treated Paganism as more of a pastime than a religion. I knew from experience that such a simple beginning could root itself and grow into a lifelong passion. I regularly got into long discussions with many of them and several remain close friends to this day.

It was also while working there that I was finally exposed to the Pagan community and discovered my passion for organizing Pagan events. I had pursued my Pagan interests on my own and many times I had wished I had more contacts who could offer advice and answer questions. As I got to know the community, I felt the need to create opportunities for new Pagans to meet other like-minded people, so they wouldn't have to muddle through alone as I did.

The first event I ever organized was a Pagan picnic in May of 2002. It was held in Central Park, Burlington, at a temporary labyrinth. This event allowed me to take my first step out of the broom closet as I went to City Hall and got a permit to use the park. I was so nervous. When the secretary asked why I needed it, I stumbled through a vague reference to May Day, to which she responded, "Oh, is this a Wiccan event?" with a smile on her face. I was instantly put at ease.

I truly believe that this experience was a pivotal moment in my development as a Pagan organizer. Had that secretary been resistant or intolerant, I may never have had the courage to continue getting permits and organizing public events. It was because of her openness and acceptance that, over the following two years, every time I organized a ritual on public property or planned picnics and other events, I always got a city permit, even when it wasn't necessary. It was my way of showing pride in my faith and my practice and it also put new people at ease, as they seemed more comfortable attending an event recognized by the city.

My organizational undertakings weren't limited to Ontario. After the success of my first picnic, I decided to organize a picnic in Moncton to see what kind of Pagan community existed in my hometown. I got in touch with a few people via e-mail who helped organize it by printing and posting flyers. On the day, I arrived at the location not knowing what to expect. By that afternoon we had over a dozen people in attendance. They came from various parts of New Brunswick, and many were extremely happy to meet other like-minded individuals. It was awesome to see and it brought people together who had thought they were alone in their beliefs, which was the whole point! As far as I know, the group maintained contact after I left and the community began to flourish.

These days, I keep myself extremely busy. I became the coordinator for Hamilton's Pagan Pride Day in 2003. One of the benefits to being the chairperson is the requirement that I be out of the broom closet. I use no pseudonym when I advertise PPD, fax press releases, or speak to reporters. I have never allowed myself to hide who I am and I have been lucky enough to have never felt as though I had no choice but to do so. I am always up front about who I am and what I'm doing.

Hamilton PPD, as well as every other event I organize, is meant to promote tolerance, offer correct information about Paganism to the public, and bring our Pagan community together. Our committee has created and molded it to be an event where those new to Paganism can feel comfortable asking questions, where the public can feel welcome walking the grounds and can see for themselves what we are and what we are not, and where Pagans can feel at ease and bring their family members along with them to celebrate the day. The only way we can clear up misconceptions and ignorance is by showing ourselves and our practice in public. Our festival is open to anyone who wishes to enter into respectful dialogue about Paganism. I strongly believe that bridges built to bring people together must be built from both ends and are two-way.

In October 2008, I and three other members of our community started the Hammertown Pagan Pub Moot, a monthly event that draws people from across Southern Ontario. In its initial five months, the success of this moot has proven to be remarkable and overwhelming! Our attendance has hovered around one hundred people every month, with our largest moot drawing almost two hundred, filling the pub almost to capacity. Everyone is delighted to be there and we have had non-Pagans comment that they've never seen such a happy crowd nor heard so much laughter and joy. From the raffle prizes donated every month, to the amount of networking and socializing that takes place, our community has completely blown me away with its enthusiasm and generosity.

Although much of my time is used to organize events, I always find time to carry on with my own personal growth. I am a member of two circles, both of which play a huge part in satisfying my commitment to lifelong learning. Simultaneously, I study the religion of ancient Egypt and apply such principles to my own private practice.

My family continues to live on the east coast and I visit them annually. Although we tend to avoid religious discussions, they respect my views and opinions. I am successful in my career, I am happy with my life, and I am a good person. There isn't much more one could ask for.

Regardless of how busy my schedule becomes, our Pagan community remains my focus and my passion. I want to do all I can to bring people together and move us forward into what I believe will be a bright future! I attend other events around Southern Ontario, including various pub moots, fundraising events, and festivals to show my support and if I could, I'd travel across Canada to attend even more. I have met so many wonderful people and I do my best to maintain and care for the friendships I have gained along the way.

As I consider my position in my community today, I am awed and humbled. There are some amazing Pagans in this world and I am honored to call many of them my friends.

THE DARK GODDESS

by Meri Fowler

I drive through the eerie darkness of a city of three million people. There are no lights, no sounds, no traffic signals, no streetlights, and no cars. I feel as if I am in a horror movie.

It's 1997, and Montreal is experiencing what we have come to call simply "The Ice Storm." Freezing rain buildup has knocked out the power in many of the areas of the city, and frigid temperatures have forced people to flee from their homes to take refuge in shelters. My name is Meri, and I am a nurse mobilized as part of the emergency services. I am also a practicing Witch.

On this night I am driving through the silent streets praying to the Dark Goddess—the Goddess of Night—that I will reach a shelter in a Jewish synagogue where I will be the medical professional in charge for twelve hours, taking care of Jewish seniors who have been evacuated from nursing homes and private residences.

I arrive at the synagogue, the only building I have seen lit up in my forty-five minute drive. Accompanied by the hum of generators volunteers have set up rows and rows of cots to make a dormitory.

People are also sleeping on the floor, on couches, and on chairs. The lights are dim, and most areas of the synagogue are silent except for the sound of snoring and coughing. I receive my report from the day nurse and meet the social worker who is spending the night caring for the people in the shelter with me. We hear screaming upstairs, and rush to find out what is going on. Many of the seniors here during the storm are Holocaust survivors, some with Alzheimer's disease. They are housed here because of the kosher kitchen that can prepare food according to their religious beliefs. The atmosphere is tense as they flash back to other forced evacuations that many of their families did not survive. The screamer is having a nightmare. We calm her and reassure her that all is well; she will be going home soon.

The long, slow hours pass as we walk gently among the sleeping people. To the ones who can't sleep, we bring warm drinks, more blankets, and try to comfort them with a few words. As night becomes early morning, it seems that everyone has finally settled down to his or her personal dreams. I take a break with Naomi, the social worker working with me. She is a strong woman in her forties, typically Jewish looking with a strong beautiful face and dramatic eyes. We talk about the emotional pain that this environmental crisis has brought to the people in the shelter, and as the quiet night settles around us our conversation turns to other holocausts and religions. Naomi tells me that she has a degree in Religion and that her husband is actually the mayor of this town, a suburb of Montreal. She asks me if I'm Jewish. Do Jewish people have red hair and freckles?

I have been Wiccan for about five years by now, and I belong to an eclectic Wiccan coven as well as participating in the Pagan community. At work I am still in the broom closet. My heart beats a little faster as the dark, quiet night weaves its spell around me. I can't bring myself to be superficial with this intense woman, as passionate about her own faith as I am about mine. "I'm Wiccan," I tell her, "a Witch." Her eyes widen just a little bit. "Wicca? I don't know about that, can you explain?"

How do we put into words the incredibly deep experiences that we have in circle, in our solitary rituals, in our conversations with the Goddess? How can we express the feeling of finding the Horned God under a full moon, feeling His presence in the spiral dance? I try to explain that Wicca is a Neo-Pagan faith with roots in pre-Christian beliefs from the British Isles. I talk about the Sabbats, the Rede, and coven. She listens intently, frowning slightly. I have never tried to explain my religion to anyone else before, let alone someone as scholarly and religious as her. I feel inadequate. My words stumble along, and I think that I must sound childish compared to her holy books, her rabbis, and her intense faith. I stop talking. She says, "I don't understand. How can this be a religion? You have no temples, no bible, no congregations, no religious leaders and no money!"

What can I say?

In the shadows behind her I feel the presence of the Goddess smiling. "Help!" I plead silently. "This is an organic religion," I tell her, "a religion of the people from heart to heart; a faith that finds the presence of the Divine within life, and nature, and ourselves. We don't have teachers and books because we are our own teachers, and our book is the sacred book of the Earth. We believe that we can connect with the God and Goddess and hear their voices, receive their inspiration directly and take responsibility for our own actions, without the intermediary of a pope or rabbi. We have a loose set of beliefs and morals and a ritual structure that is common to all Wiccans, but there is room for creativity and deep mystical experiences. This is a faith with roots as old as the earth."

She stops for a moment and considers, smiling slightly as if trying to imagine a religion as free as ours, where joy and pleasure are prayer and women are equal to men. She shakes her head a little as if the concept of what we are is almost too radical. Then she smiles, and says, "It sounds beautiful!"

Since that day, I have never been afraid to come out of the broom closet and tell people that I am Wiccan. My husband and I were asked to give a little course on the basics at an esoteric type store near our house, and after nine weeks the group with us refused to leave! We formed a coven with them based on our study and our training, Celtic Shamanic Wicca. More people heard about us and asked for classes. Our original students took their own students, who grew and changed and started to teach themselves. We opened a Wiccan community center and even more people started coming! It's been twelve years since the ice storm, and our community has spread, grown, and matured. I have met wonderful dynamic and inspired people as well as liars and fakes, but mostly it has been an experience of coming home, of finding my people and of manifesting the Goddess. I think of Naomi from time to time, and I wonder if she thinks of me. At last I have realized what that night was all about. The Dark Goddess, the hidden truth of our path, was speaking to me through Naomi. It was her I met on that long, dark night, not a social worker asking questions. I faced the test: "Do you believe in me?" And I passed.

CALLED TO WALK A PUBLIC PATH: WORKING THROUGH THE CHALLENGE OF SHYNESS

by Arin Murphy-Hiscock

I am extremely fortunate in that my discovery, adoption, and subsequent activity within Wicca hasn't been difficult for me. There have certainly been pointed comments made about it by various people, but most of them were made to friends, not to my face. In fact, the proverbial stars have seemed to align every step of the way as if to reassure me that my path is indeed the right one for me to be traveling.

To begin with, I didn't have a huge breakup with my original religion, or a dramatic discovery of alternate spirituality. I was casually raised in the Anglican Church, and I backed away when demands on my time and energy for too many extracurricular church projects forced me into a corner when I was a teenager. I was dreadfully shy and never a big joiner to begin with, so when pressed by so many authoritarian adults to join various committees and groups, I just faded out of the congregation. My mother wasn't far behind me, either, for similar reasons.

About ten years went by. I became engaged to a man who was a fervent Christian, which I fully supported as right for him. I began to feel that familiar social pressure again when he persuaded me to accompany him to church regularly, and even more so when the priest who agreed to marry us set as one of his criteria the full commitment to a parish for both of us.

Around this time I also became involved in a joint storytelling project among my friends that was exploring the paranormal. I decided that the character I would introduce into the story would be a modern witch. The man organizing the project, a dear friend, told me about an esoteric bookstore that I should check out to get a good overview of modern witchcraft. I bought three books and read them in two days, then went back to get more. Far beyond simple background research, the material I read spoke to me in a very personal way. The Divine in Nature? A female aspect as well as a male aspect of God? Multiple expressions of both those aspects of the Divine? These were concepts that made a lot of sense to me. While my fiancé knew what I was researching, he didn't oppose it, as he was part of the same project. Nor did he suspect that it was working upon me at a very deep level.

Our engagement was dissolved six weeks before the wedding date, for reasons other than religion, although I do admit to a sense of relief when I realized that my spirituality wouldn't have to be a point of contention between us sometime in the future.

One of the most attractive aspects of this new spiritual path was that I was free to follow it alone, and worship solitarily. I slowly slipped into a more actively Pagan way of life. I followed the moon cycles with more awareness; I began to do small private rituals; and I began wearing a tiny pentacle on a long chain around my neck, always hidden beneath my shirt.

I worked in a speculative fiction bookstore right down the street from the occult shop, and while some of the clientele overlapped, there was a vocal anti–New Age portion of the specific readers who regularly bashed the esoterics; it was a sport of sorts. Common sense in a customer-focused industry dictates that you don't take sides, because no matter what you do you'll end up offending someone. Beyond that, however, my faith was still new enough that I wanted to keep it private. I kept my head down for a few months, then began to allow myself to be drawn into the conversations, and inserted a few neutral comments here and there—nothing overt, just fair. And then one day, one of the customers turned to me and said jovially, "But of course you're much too intelligent to get caught up in all that incense-soaked witchy stuff!"

"Actually," I said calmly, "I'm Wiccan."

You could have heard a pin drop. There was, I admit, a part of me that tasted satisfaction when I saw the sudden fear and shame play over their faces as each of them went back over the things they'd said in my presence over the last few months. "Oh," one of them said inadequately, and the subject was quickly altered. There was another part of me that felt incredibly buoyant and liberated. The rush of adrenaline that flooded my body when I spoke came as a surprise to me. It was the first time I had ever mentioned it to anyone, or even spoken the words aloud to myself. My own physical and emotional reactions confirmed that I was committed to this path.

A week or so later, one by one the people who had been part of that conversation trickled in at different times to ask me about the Neo-Pagan thing. Each of them left thinking that maybe it wasn't so dizzy after all if someone so obviously grounded and well-educated talked about it so, well, normally.

After that I wasn't so paranoid about letting the pentacle slip out from under my sweater when I bent to pick up a box, and wasn't as careful about hiding my reading material at lunch. Over the next few years I read piles of books and began to practice more and more. A year or two after my public claiming of my path, feeling slightly disconnected and wondering if what I was doing was common, I registered for an introductory course. At the end of it the teacher looked at me and said, "Why are you here? You should be teaching this stuff. You know so much about it." And that's precisely what I did: I began to teach with her. And when the speculative fiction bookshop closed I was immediately hired at the occult store, and would end up as assistant manager there before I officially left retail a few years down the road.

My family was a different matter. My parents lived in a different city, and religion had never been a huge presence in our lives. I believe that one's choice of faith is a personal thing and requires no sanction by family, especially if everyone's an adult. My faith was my business. Wicca is a way of life, and I was perfectly happy to live it without broadcasting it until one day while on a visit I was talking to my mother and she said something that caught my attention. It was a turn of phrase that only someone reading Pagan material would have used; I don't even remember what it was now. In turn I dropped a reference of my own, and she heard me and dropped yet another reference, until finally I said, "Mum, have you been reading Pagan stuff?" It turned out that she had. The synchronicity was delicious for both of us! It made it a lot easier when I started showing up in the newspaper and on TV as a local specialist and consultant about the topic. My father, on the other hand, fretted about what my grandmother would think if she found out. In the end, my mother casually left a book on reincarnation on the coffee table when my grandmother visited them from across the country. Naturally my grandmother noticed it, and to everyone's surprise declared herself to be a believer in the phenomenon. She turned out to have interesting ideas of her own about spirituality and the afterlife, and my mother finally told her about my religious practice. My mother later reported to me that my grandmother seemed quite interested in the whole concept and agreed with several of the principles. She even confided a few stories about the Sight popping up in our ancestry, something we never would have known otherwise. Suddenly the deep dark family secret wasn't so dark after all!

My peers were very accepting; in fact, some of them had done their own personal research into Neo-Paganism at various times. My religious choices have never been a source of tension or misunderstanding among us—we respect one another's choices and philosophies. However, the day after my first interview was prominently published in the major local paper (complete with a large photo!) I had a dinner date with my new fiancé at his parents' house, and I was concerned. My new fiancé had been shopping at the occult store long before I had and his parents were familiar with his own free-form alternative spirituality with a shamanic focus, but this was, perhaps, different. What would they say about it? How would they react? It wasn't until dessert when one of them brought the article up, and of course everything was fine: they were genuinely interested in what I did and what my thoughts were about spirituality and religion in general.

Ultimately, I'm very happy with how slowly and naturally Paganism entwined through my life, and how and when I chose to share the information with others. I don't define myself solely by my spiritual path; it's simply a part of me and my life, albeit a large part. However, I am thankful that it has become such a deeply essential part of who I am. I've had the opportunity to meet some wonderful people, learn some very interesting things, undergo life-changing experiences, and expand my career in an unanticipated direction because of it. Helping to establish a publishing imprint, guide its development, and ultimately write books about the practice of nature-based alternative spirituality were experiences I'd never dreamed about, but my involvement in the book industry and my knowledge of alternative spirituality led me jointly to where I am today.

Writing about spirituality has led me to examine it in ways I possibly never would otherwise have done, and has deepened and refined my own practice and beliefs. And every time I receive a letter or an email from a reader who says "Thank you, you have helped me define what I have been feeling" or "You have inspired me," I know that what I am doing and what I practice are doing good in the world. And ultimately, that is one of the greatest blessings my public admission that day in the bookstore over thirteen years ago has led to.

It is ironic that my calling has turned out to involve being such a public figure, as I am a very shy and introverted individual. This, then, has been my ultimate challenge. I walk a path that is perhaps more public than others; I teach, lecture, lead workshops, and publish books on the subject. Each of my public appearances is in essence another step out of the figurative broom closet for me. My timidity makes it hard to do, but my spiritual connection to my gods and my path give me strength. I celebrate my relationship with the Goddess and God, and pray for guidance as I do my public work, and trust that I am following the vocation the gods have created for me.

Everyone's path is different. The steps taken along it, from private to public practitioner, are also varied, and the challenges each of us face are unique. Communicating our beliefs and commitment to that path is one such challenge, one that comes at a different stage of the journey for everyone. I doubt I'll ever shake the feeling that I'm telling people I'm Pagan for the first time. I do know that by reaffirming it anew every time, I am publicly identifying myself as a follower of a rich, personal, and joyful spiritual path, and reminding myself of the fact as well.

CONTRIBUTORS

ᛰ **KRISTEN ADAMS** is a forty-two-year-old wife, Witch, and mother of five children. She became disabled in 2004 while teaching a special needs class and has since devoted her life to raising her family and practicing the Craft in Hollis, NH.

ᛰ **SHOSHANA E. BERMAN** Is a retired nurse living in Tampa, FL. She volunteers at the Big Brothers/Big Sisters Organization and the local Hospice Organization in the Center for Grieving Children. She also enjoys sewing and quilting.

ᛰ **BLADE** can usually be found in his native habitat of online games, or trying to design his own. He has been spotted in the wild warding for public rituals, and at home trying to herd the four cats he rents living space from.

ᛰ **GREGORY MICHAEL BREWER** has been a student and practitioner of the Craft for over sixteen years. He is a third degree initiate and is a cofounder of an eclectic Wiccan study group called The Circle of the Spirit Tree. Gregory lives in Bloomington, IL, and is currently working on his bachelor's in English while revising his first novel.

ᛰ **MAEL BRIGDE** lives in Vancouver, BC, Canada, where she writes fiction under the name C. June Wolf. Her short story collection *Finding Creatures & Other Stories* was released in September 2008. She is a frequent traveler to Haiti and lives quite happily in a single room with two odd, but even-tempered, cats.

ᛰ **BOB CHIPMAN**, a resident of Saco, ME, was ordained by a small circle called the Forest Sanctuary in Southern Maine. Using his magical name, Greywolf Moonsong, Bob hosts a podcast called "A Pagan Heart in Maine." He lives with his wonderful wife, Sandy, their roommate, Alta, and their two cats.

- ✎ **TRACEY COSTA** lives in Wareham, MA, with her husband and children and works at the University of Massachusetts, Dartmouth. Tracey recognizes how blessed she is to have the loving embrace of the God and Goddess, her family, and her Wiccan group, which have all given her the courage to worship while healing her mind, soul, and body.

- ✎ **JUNIOR CRONE** has studied Paganism academically since 1998, having completed a Bachelor of Arts in Anthropology at Concordia University in Montreal in 2001, and more recently a master's degree in Religious Studies, Anthropology of Religion, at the University of Ottawa in 2008. She has authored articles on how the interplay of gender, sexual politics, ethnicity, and language affect the development of Paganism in the bilingual city of Montreal, Quebec, Canada. An occasional blogger, she is currently in the process of adapting her master's thesis on Paganism in Montreal into a book.

- ✎ **SANDI DUNHAM** has been a member of the Correllian Nativist Church International for over ten years. She drives a school bus and resides in Nassau, NY, with her husband, Rick, and two children, Andrew and Samantha.

- ✎ **GINA ELLIS** was born in 1936 in Calgary, Alberta, Canada, and currently lives near the town of Perth, one hundred kilometers west of Ottawa. She has two daughters, one who lives next door and the other who works for Wizards of the Coast in Seattle, WA. She has held various occupations, mainly as an office slave but including a fun period as a junk dealer. Now widowed and retired, she is concentrating on gardening and doing some traveling, such as to the ruins of old Goddess cultures in Malta and Turkey. Her (mostly non-Pagan) blog can be found at *http://open.salon.com/blog/myriad*.

- ✎ **HIGH PRIESTESS ENOCH** lives in North Charleston, SC. She is a Druid and Wiccan High Priestess. Enoch is a member of a nationally recognized CUPPS Chapter and leads her own circle called the Mystics. She can be contacted at *PsychicSpellCaster.com*.

- ✎ **MERI FOWLER** has been a Wiccan since 1992, has studied a variety of traditions, and belongs to a Celtic Shamanic Wiccan Coven in Montreal, Quebec, Canada. She has been studying Shamanism with the Foundation for Shamanic Studies since 2003 and animating the Young Pagan's Circle since September 2000, creating a place where young people between the ages of ten and eighteen can explore alternative spirituality. Meri has a Bachelor of Science in Nursing and has been a nurse since 1986. She has a second dan in Ninjitsu, and currently works full time as a palliative care nurse.

ↀ **TONI PEEBLES FRANKS** is a thirty-five-year-old singer, harpist, chandler, herb gardener and recent college graduate. She lives in Somerville, Alabama, with her husband of fourteen years and their two children.

ↀ **BRENDA GIBSON** has been a solitary practitioner for four years and has practiced with a group for two years. She raised three children in Ohio, one of which also follows the Wiccan path. She currently resides in Marshfield, MA, with her fiancé, Bill.

ↀ **MICHAEL GLEASON** was initiated into Wicca in 1974, earning the rank of High Priest in 1977. He joined Witches Against Religious Discrimination several years ago, and has been active working on educating the public for many years. He is active with the Witches Education Bureau in Salem, MA, and was formerly the coeditor and publisher of *THiNK!* magazine. A resident of Beverly, MA, Michael spends his free time reading and writing reviews of esoteric books for a variety of publishers.

ↀ **DEB GOESCHEL** lives, works, plays, and practices many things in southeastern Massachusetts, Rhode Island, and the greater New England area, including web communications, yoga instruction and practice, writing, hiking mountains, level III Reiki, ESM (Environmental Stress Management), IET (Integrated Energy Therapy), singing Irish tunes every chance she gets, reading Tarot cards, and eclectic/Gardnerian/Celtic/Shamanic Wicca. Deb resides in South Attleboro, MA.

ↀ **RICHARD J. GOULART** is a graduate of Massachusetts College of Art and Design and is currently working on at least a half-dozen graphic novels, as well as other art, writing, music, and video projects. He is a member and advisor of an established Wiccan group and lives in Middleborough, MA, with his wife, Mary, and two children, Dylan and Jason.

ↀ **DELIA E. HALNEN-ON** has been a member of an established Wiccan group for the past two years. She is a customer-service representative and resides in Plymouth, MA, with her husband, Jack, and her mother, Jan.

∾ **BONNIE S. HANN** lives in Ft. Loudon, PA, with her husband, Scott, and three children, Rashaun, Destiny and Scott Hann, Jr. She works as a receptionist and has been a proud Witch for several years.

∾ **WALTER R. HARDIN, JR.** lives in Kearney, NE. He is a full time student at Central Community College aspiring to start his own photography business. He lives with his wife, Nancy, and has four children, Anthony, Zackery, Alisha, and Cordell.

∾ **DEIRDRE ANNE HEBERT** lives in Dover, NH. She is the host of *PaganFM*, which airs on WSCA-LP in Portsmouth, NH. Also, she and a small group of like-minded people are currently founding Qh4u, a LGBT telephone hotline. She is a musician, poet, and an aspiring photographer.

∾ **JOHN DAVID HICKEY** is originally from Quebec City and has lived in Montreal since the spring of 1993. He's a professional and published writer, working as a technical writer by day and telling tales as a storyteller by night. In February of 2005, he published his first book/CD of stories called *You Don't Know Jack*. In terms of his own spiritual path, it's a long and winding one. Not content with any one path or tradition, he explores freely, finding truth and enlightenment in a variety of cultures and perspectives. Hobbes is currently the president of the Montreal Pagan Resource Centre and believes in providing opportunities and offering choices to the local Pagan community.

∾ **AMANDA HYDE** has been organizing Pagan events in Southern Ontario since 2002, including moots, fundraisers and open rituals. She is the coordinator of Hamilton Pagan Pride Day and is one of the founding board members for the Hammertown Pagan Pub Moot. In her mundane life, Amanda works as a sign-language interpreter. She has also been writing short stories, novels, and poetry since she was eight years old and had her first teen fiction novel published in 2001. She lives in Hamilton, Ontario, Canada, with her two cats, Toast and Jelly, and her bearded dragon, Vincent.

∾ **ICINIA** is a natural Kitchen Witch who was born and raised near Montreal, Quebec, Canada. Her belief is that a healthy spiritual life begins at home and is maintained by close family ties, daily communication with Nature, good food and, of course, a busy, happy kitchen!

ᕙ **JEFFREY JARVIS** lives quietly, looking for the moments that teach him the deeper meaning of happiness in everyday life, and for ways to remind others of the love inherent in the world. He currently lives in Burton, OH, where he explores the woods with his children, works on the family farm, and plans excursions to visit dear friends, climb mountains, and sample cider. He's still flying, and figures that's a pretty decent baseline from which to reach out, explore the world, and deepen his experience.

ᕙ **JESSICA JENKINS** first discovered and began to explore Paganism over twelve years ago. Since then, she has continued on to become a third-level graduate of The Crescent Moon School. Currently, Jessica is a second degree High Priestess studying with a private coven associated with the Black Forest Circle and Seminary. She is also a co-founder of Gealach Dorcha, a group which designs workshops and rituals for women, by women.

ᕙ **CERRIDWEN JOHNSON** was born and raised in a Gardnerian coven. At twenty-five years old she is a first degree Gardnerian initiate and a Peace Corps volunteer in Africa. Cerridwen is from Banjul, The Gambia, West Africa.

ᕙ **ELENA M. KELLEY** lives in Quincy, MA, and has been practicing Wicca since 1999. Her first coven was of the Dianic tradition. She left that coven in 2000 and became a solitary witch until 2006, when she was introduced to a High Priestess and became a member of an established Wiccan congregation. She also performs as a Bard.

ᕙ **ERYNN ROWAN LAURIE** is a writer and professional madwoman who has been a part of the Pagan community since 1984. One of the many founders of the Celtic Reconstructionist Pagan movement, she is passionately interested in world religions, history, spirituality, and a great variety of other topics. Her website is *www.seanet.com/~inisglas*. She lives in Everett, WA.

ᕙ **MARY LAVOIE** is proprietress of Crescent Moon Herbals, a unique shop that offers a variety of metaphysical services, workshops, and gifts. Crescent Moon Herbals actively participates in fund-raising events for several charitable organizations. Mary Lavoie resides in Lebanon, ME, with her husband Jerry and their four children.

ᕙ **LYNETTE C. MANSANI** is an administrative support receptionist for a nonprofit agency that helps people in financial need. She attends Bridgewater

State College part time, majoring in Anthropology and Public Archaeology. Lynette has been a member of an established Wiccan congregation since August of 2006 and lives in Plymouth, MA, with her son Aidan.

☙ PAUL MCVICKER is a twenty-eight-year-old student nurse. He lives in Antrim Town in Northern Ireland.

☙ AMY MIDNIGHT lives with her Muslim family in Singapore. Her greatest aspiration is to move to California and live with her sister Cassandra.

☙ ASTARTE MOONSILVER is both a member of the Iowa Organization of Wiccans and Neo-Pagans and the Sisters of the Goddess. She also holds Sabbat observances with South Central Iowa Pagan Alliance, a group that she started in December 2006. She lives in Chariton, IA, with her five children.

☙ BRENDAN MYERS is the author of several well-respected philosophy books, including *The Other Side of Virtue* and *A Pagan Testament*. He earned his PhD in philosophy from the National University of Ireland, and currently lectures at the University of Guelph.

☙ ASHLEEN O'GAEA has fond memories of her native Pacific Northwest, but now calls Arizona home. She is among the founding members of the Tucson Area Wiccan-Pagan Network (TAWN), a cofounder of Adventure Wicca, and the senior-writing Priestess for Mother Earth Ministries-ATC, a Neo-Pagan prison ministry. She and her husband Canyondancer teach, lecture, present workshops, and perform a wide range of passage rites. They live northwest of Tucson, AZ, with three cats and a thirteen-year-old puppy.

☙ OISCE is an Australian writer who has had a variety of work published, including a verse novel, short stories, poems, feature articles, and, in 2003, *Sunwyse: Celebrating the Sacred Wheel of the Year in Australia*. She both studies and teaches writing and literature at a tertiary level. An intense interest in religion and spirituality has seen her explore many world views, but it's the path of earth-based spirituality that she has chosen to walk. Her practice has included time spent in Ireland exploring her Celtic heritage, learning about folk wisdom, mythology, literature, and the oral art of storytelling.

☙ ANDA POWERS has been an eclectic Wiccan for more than a decade. Her poetry and prose have appeared in many publications, and she is currently promoting her latest book, *Amae: The Pagan Woman's Guide to Intimacy*. Anda and her husband live in Knoxville, TN. She can be contacted through her website: *www.andapowers.com.*

⟶ **STEVEN PRINCE** was born and raised near Melbourne, Australia. He graduated from Deakin University in Australia in 2003 with a degree in economics and human resources management. Currently, he is working in Human Resources for an international hiring firm while planning to move to the United States to be with his fiancée, Elena.

⟶ **GWINEVERE RAIN** is a Wiccan practitioner who currently resides in Florida. She is the author of three nonfiction books for teens, *Spellcraft for Teens, Moonbeams & Shooting Stars,* and *Confessions of a Teenage Witch.* She runs *Copper Moon* E-zine (*www.copper-moon.com*), an online magazine for Wiccans in their teens and twenties.

⟶ **IDRIL ROGERS** is fifty-three years old and lives in a small town in Wiltshire, England, with her husband. She is the mother of three and grandmother of seven, a part-time care worker, and an Elder and High Priestess of a multifaith ministry that is a registered charity in the United Kingdom.

⟶ **ROB ST. MARTIN** is a Montreal-born-and -bred author, editor, illustrator, graphic designer, actor, singer, and, like many authors, has held numerous interesting jobs in his life. Ask him sometime, he'll be happy to tell you all about them. He has been following his Pagan path for ten years. His publications include articles, reviews, short stories, and novels. Additionally, he coedited the fantasy anthology *Ages Of Wonder,* published by DAW in March 2009. Though he has nothing against them, he does not live with cats, despite having done so in the past. He can be found online at *www.talyesin.com.*

⟶ **DEBRA SIEGRIST** lives in the countryside of Higganum, CT, where she enjoys gardening and writing poetry. She lives with her husband, youngest son, and dog named Laci.

⟶ **TARAS STASIUK** is a lifelong Montrealer who recently moved to a six-acre homestead situated somewhere between that city and Ottawa, Canada. He calls his highly personal path Performance Shamanism, the first word reflecting his use of live theatrical and musical performance, in addition to his writing. The goal of Performance Shamanism is to help people to do what it is they're here on Earth to do, primarily through inspiration and example.

In order to heal, however, you must attack the disease, and so Taras is also a sworn hunter of nay-sayers and inner-critics.

ε∽ JOSHUA M. THOMAS from Germantown, MD, is a graphic design and electronic media major at Towson University in Baltimore, MD. He runs an online store called Skyclad Designs where he sells unique Pagan designs on apparel and merchandise, and also does volunteer work for the Open Hearth Foundation.

ε∽ PAUL TURNBULL a Duxbury, MA, resident, is a fifty-eight-year-old father of nine, freelance writer, and grocery store cashier. He has a master's degree in clinical psychology, and worked for many years as an associate psychologist and later, as a certified alcoholism counselor. More recently, he sought his fortune as an eighteen-wheel truck driver, and worked in Service to the Armed Forces for the American Red Cross at Fort Belvoir, VA, during Operations Desert Shield and Desert Storm. He is a Christian and a Witch.

ε∽ JOAN WITHINGTON is a fifty-something-year-old mother of a daughter and two sons, and also the grandmother of fourteen grandchildren. Joan is the High Priestess of the Triple Moon Coven that she and her husband Alf (aka Taliesin) run from their home in Wigan, Lancashire, England. Joan was initiated into the Craft in the mid-1980s and took over the coven in the late-1990s.

ε∽ JANICE MATHIESON WRIGHT is living her green witch path on a six-acre homestead in rural Ontario with her husband, a dog, two cats, and a flock of chickens. When she's not tending the garden, walking in the woods, baking bread, or learning to quilt, she works part-time as a freelance writer, editor, and proofreader. She has a large collection of polar fleece sweaters, drinks single-malt Scotch, and her favorite color is purple.

ε∽ CERI YOUNG started studying Paganism in 1999, but it wasn't until early 2001 that she became a practicing Wiccan. She was one of the founding members of the Montreal Pagan Resource Center and volunteered for many years as a copyeditor for the Pagan community magazine *WynterGreene*. Nowadays, she considers herself an eclectic kitchen witch and tries to bring spiritual awareness into her daily life. She lives in Montreal, Quebec, Canada, where she works as a video game writer.

ABOUT THE EDITOR

Arin Murphy-Hiscock currently lives in Montreal, Canada, where she works as a freelance writer and editor. She has been involved with Wicca and Paganism since 1995, giving classes, workshops, lectures, and interviews. She is one of the founding members of the Montreal Pagan Resource Centre, and her books include *Power Spellcraft for Life*, *Solitary Wicca for Life*, *The Way of the Green Witch*, and *The Way of the Hedge Witch*. Her website is *www.arinmurphyhiscock.com*.